First World War
and Army of Occupation
War Diary
France, Belgium and Germany

23 DIVISION
Divisional Troops
40 Sanitary Section
20 August 1915 - 1 April 1917

WO95/2180/2

The Naval & Military Press Ltd
www.nmarchive.com
Published in association with The National Archives

Published by

The Naval & Military Press Ltd

Unit 10 Ridgewood Industrial Park,

Uckfield, East Sussex,

TN22 5QE England

Tel: +44 (0) 1825 749494

www.naval-military-press.com

www.nmarchive.com

Contents

Document type	Place/Title	Date From	Date To
Heading	WO95/2180/2 20 Division-Divnl. Troops 40 Sanitary Section 1915 Aug-1917 March		
Heading	23rd Division No. 40 Sanitary Section Aug 1915-1917 Mar To 1 Army		
Heading	23rd Division Summarised but not copied No. 40 Sanitary Section (23rd Div) Vol 1 Aug & Sep 1. 15		
Heading	War Diary Of Sanitary Section 40 R.A.M.C. (T) 23 Division From August 20th 1915 To September 30th 1915 (Volume 1)		
War Diary	Chelsea	20/08/1915	20/08/1915
War Diary	London	21/08/1915	22/08/1915
War Diary	Bordon Camp	23/08/1915	28/08/1915
War Diary	Havre	28/08/1915	29/08/1915
War Diary	Tilques	30/08/1915	06/09/1915
War Diary	Renescure	07/09/1915	09/09/1915
War Diary	Merris	10/09/1915	16/09/1915
War Diary	Croix Du Bac	17/09/1915	17/09/1915
War Diary	Croix Du Bac and Erquinghem Lys	21/09/1915	30/09/1915
Heading	23rd Division 40th Sanitary Section Vol 2 Oct 15		
Heading	War Diary Of Sanitary Section 40 R.A.M.C. (T), 23rd Division From October 1st To October 31st 1915 Volume II		
War Diary	Croix Du Bac And Erquinghem Lys (Sub Section)	01/10/1915	31/10/1915
Heading	23rd Division No. 48 Jan. Sect. Vol 3 Summarised but not copied Nov 15		
Heading	War Diary Of Sanitary Section 40 R.A.M.C.T. 23rd Division From November 1st to November 30th 1915 (Volume 4)		
War Diary	Croix Du Bac And Erquinghem Lys. (Sub Section)	01/11/1915	30/11/1915
Heading	23rd Division San. Sect. 40 Vol 4 Summarised but not copied Dec 1915		
Heading	War Diary Of Sanitary Section 40 R.A.M.C.T. 23rd Division From December 1st 1915 to December 31st 1915 (Volume 4)		
War Diary	Croix du Bac and Erquingham (Sub-Section)	01/12/1915	17/12/1915
War Diary	Croix du Bac and Erquinghem	18/12/1915	31/12/1915
Heading	23rd Div. 40th July Section Jan Feb Mar April 1916		
Heading	23rd San: Sect. 40 Vol. 5		
Heading	War Diary Of 23rd Division From January 1st 1916 to January 31st 1916. (Volume 5)		
War Diary	Croix du Bac and Erquinghem (Sub Section)	01/01/1916	31/01/1916
Heading	San. Sect. 40 Vol. 6		
Heading	War Diary Of Sanitary Section 40 RAMC (T) To Division From February 1st 1916 To February 29th 1916 (Volume 6)		
War Diary	Croix du Bac and Erquinghem (Sub Section)	01/02/1916	20/02/1916
War Diary	Croix du Bac and Erquinghem Estaires Morbeque and Blaringhem	21/02/1916	29/02/1916
Miscellaneous			
Miscellaneous	Sanitary Section 23rd Division		

Heading	War Diary Of Sanitary Section 40 R.A.M.C. (T) 23rd Division From March 1st to March 31st 1916 (Volume 7)		
War Diary		01/03/1916	31/03/1916
Heading	War Diary Of Sanitary Section 40, R.A.M.C. (T) 23rd Division From 1st April 1916 To 30th April 1916 (Volume 8)		
War Diary	Headquaters and Main section at Sains En Gohelle Squads at Barlin,	01/04/1916	10/04/1916
War Diary	Bully-Grenay	11/04/1916	11/04/1916
War Diary	Aix-Noulette and Citie Calonne	12/04/1916	18/04/1916
War Diary	Bruay	19/04/1916	30/04/1916
Heading	War Diary Of Sanitary Section 40 R.A.M.C. (T) From May 1st to May 31st 1916 (Volume 9)		
War Diary	Bruay	01/05/1916	14/05/1916
War Diary	Sains En Gohelle Bully Grenay, Aix Noulette	15/05/1916	15/05/1916
War Diary	Hersin	16/05/1916	17/05/1916
War Diary	Barlin	18/05/1916	20/05/1916
War Diary	Sains En Gohelle, Bully Grenay	20/05/1916	20/05/1916
War Diary	Aix Noulette	21/05/1916	21/05/1916
War Diary	Hersin	21/05/1916	21/05/1916
War Diary	Barlin	21/05/1916	25/05/1916
War Diary	Sains-En-Gohelle	25/05/1916	26/05/1916
War Diary	Bully Grenay	26/05/1916	26/05/1916
War Diary	Aix Noulette	26/05/1916	26/05/1916
War Diary	Hersin	27/05/1916	27/05/1916
War Diary	Barlin	27/05/1916	31/05/1916
Heading	War Diary Of Sanitary Section 40 RAMCT 23rd Division From June 1st 1916 to June 30th 1916 (Volume 10)		
War Diary	Barlin	01/06/1916	05/06/1916
War Diary	Boyeffles	06/06/1916	14/06/1916
War Diary	Bruay	14/06/1916	16/06/1916
War Diary	Bomy	16/06/1916	25/06/1916
War Diary	Vaux	25/06/1916	30/06/1916
Heading	War Diary 28 Sanitary Section 40, R.A.M.C.T 23rd Division (Volume 11)		
War Diary	Vaux	01/07/1916	01/07/1916
War Diary	Baizieux	02/07/1916	04/07/1916
War Diary	Dernancourt	04/07/1916	08/07/1916
War Diary	Fricourt	09/07/1916	11/07/1916
War Diary	St Gratien	11/07/1916	21/07/1916
War Diary	Henencourt	21/07/1916	26/07/1916
War Diary	Albert	26/07/1916	31/07/1916
Heading	23rd Div. War Diary Of Sanitary Section 40 R.A.M.C. (1) From August 1st To August 31st 1916 (Volume 12)		
War Diary	Albert	01/08/1916	07/08/1916
War Diary	(Albert) To Baizieux	08/08/1916	08/08/1916
War Diary	Baizieux	09/08/1916	10/08/1916
War Diary	Baizieux To Ailly-Le-Haut-Clocher	11/08/1916	11/08/1916
War Diary	Ailly-Le-Haut-Clocher	12/08/1916	12/08/1916
War Diary	Ailly Le Haut Clocher To Baileul	13/08/1916	13/08/1916
War Diary	Fletre	14/08/1916	16/08/1916
War Diary	Fletre To Steenwerck	17/08/1916	17/08/1916
War Diary	Steenwerck	18/05/1916	22/08/1916
War Diary	Steenwerck To Near Pont's Achelles	23/08/1916	28/08/1916

War Diary		29/09/1916	29/09/1916
War Diary	F. Cav reported for duty Used in Morning but not Afternoon	30/09/1916	30/09/1916
War Diary	F. Cav Used Morning & Afternoon	31/08/1916	31/08/1916
Heading	War Diary Of O.C. 40th Sanitary Section R.A.M.C. (T) 23rd Division (September 1916) (Volume 13)		
War Diary	(Ploegsteert Area)	01/09/1916	01/09/1916
War Diary	Pont & Achelles	01/09/1916	05/09/1916
War Diary	Pont D Achelles	06/09/1916	06/09/1916
War Diary	(Ploegsteert Area) To Tilques	06/09/1916	09/09/1916
War Diary	Tilques To Allonville	10/09/1916	11/09/1916
War Diary	Allonville To Baizieux	12/09/1916	30/09/1916
Heading	War Diary Of The 40 Sanitary Section, R.A.M.C. (T) 23rd Div (from October 1st To October 31st 1916) (Volume 14)		
War Diary	Baizieux	01/10/1916	08/10/1916
War Diary	Baizieux To Montigny	09/10/1916	09/10/1916
War Diary	Montigny	10/10/1916	11/10/1916
War Diary	Montigny To Ailly Le Haut-Clocher	12/10/1916	12/10/1916
War Diary	Ailly-Le-Haut-Clocher To St Riquer	13/10/1916	15/10/1916
War Diary	From St Riquier To Poperinghe	15/10/1916	31/10/1916
Heading	War Diary Of O.C. 40 Sanitary Section R.A.M.C. T 23rd Division (Volume 15)		
War Diary	Ypres Salient Nr Poperinghe	01/11/1916	19/11/1916
War Diary	20th see next Sheet	21/11/1916	30/11/1916
Heading	War Diary Of O.C To Sanitary Section, R.A.M.C. (T) From December 1st To December 31st 1916 (Volume 16)		
War Diary		02/12/1916	31/12/1916
Heading	War Diary Of O.C 40 Sanitary Section R.A.M.C. (T.F) (Volume 17) (January 1st 1917 To January 31st 1917)		
War Diary	Ypres (Sector)	01/01/1917	31/01/1917
Heading	War Diary Of O.C. 40 Sanitary Section R.A.M.C. (T) (February 1st to February 28th 1917) (Volume 18)		
War Diary	Near Poperinghe	01/02/1917	26/02/1917
War Diary	Houlle	26/02/1917	28/02/1917
Heading	War Diary O.C. Sanitary. Section 40 March 1917 Vol 19		
War Diary	Houlle	01/03/1917	19/03/1917
War Diary	Houlle To Esquelbecq	19/03/1917	01/04/1917

WO 95 2180 /2

20 Division - Divnl. Troops

40 SANITARY SECTION

1915 AUG - 1917 MARCH

23RD DIVISION

NO.40 SANITARY SECTION

AUG 1915-~~DEC 1916~~ 1917 MAR

TO 1 ARMY

S

23rd Division

Summarised but not copied

121/6997

Aug + Sept 1915

No: 40 Sanitary Section (23rd Div)

Vol I

Aug + Sept 15.

Aug '15
Dec '16

CONFIDENTIAL

WAR DIARY OF

SANITARY SECTION 40 R.A.M.C(T) 23 Division

from August 20th 1915 to September 30th 1915

(VOLUME I)

E J Messent
Lieut RAMC (T)
O.C. Sanitary Section 40

Instructions regarding War Diaries and Intelligence Summaries are contained in F. S. Regs., Part II. and the Staff Manual respectively. Title Pages will be prepared in manuscript.

WAR DIARY
or
INTELLIGENCE SUMMARY

(Erase heading not required.)

Army Form C. 2118

Place	Date	Hour	Summary of Events and Information	Remarks and references to Appendices
CHELSEA, LONDON	August 20th '15	8.30 am	Section left LONDON to join Division at BORDON, Hants. EJM	
BORDON CAMP.	21st 22nd 23rd 24th 25th 26th		Instruction in sanitation and clearing up camps. EJM	
	27th		Section entrained at BORDON at 1.5 pm. for SOUTHAMPTON; arrived at SOUTHAMPTON DOCKS 3.0 pm; embarked on "S.S. VIPER" 5.30 pm. EJM	
	28th	6.0 am.	Section disembarked at HAVRE EJM	
HAVRE	28th	7.0 pm.	Section entrained with other units. EJM	
	29th	3.0 pm.	Arrived at ST. OMER, and marched to TILQUES arriving at billet in latter village at 5.0 pm. EJM	
TILQUES	30th 31st		Section employed in general sanitary duties. EJM	

1875 Wt. W593/826 1,000,000 4/15 J.B.C. & A. A.D.S.S./Forms/C. 2118.

Instructions regarding War Diaries and Intelligence Summaries are contained in F. S. Regs., Part II. and the Staff Manual respectively. Title Pages will be prepared in manuscript.

WAR DIARY
or
INTELLIGENCE SUMMARY
(Erase heading not required.)

Army Form C. 2118

Place	Date	Hour	Summary of Events and Information	Remarks and references to Appendices
	SEPTEMBER			
TILQUES	1st – 5th		Section employed in general sanitary duties.	EJm
	5th		Orders received to depart from TILQUES	EJm
	6th	10.0 am	Section joined up with other units and proceeded on the march to RENESCURE; arrived RENESCURE 4.30 pm	EJm
RENESCURE	7th	8.0 am	Departed from RENESCURE and marched to MERRIS, arriving at latter place at 5.30 pm.	EJm
MERRIS	8th – 15th		Section employed on general sanitary duties	EJm
	12th		O.C. proceeded to ERQUINGHEM LYS with N.C.O. to meet O.C. Sanitary Section, 24th Division and take over billet	EJm
	15th		Received orders to depart from MERRIS	EJm

1875 Wt. W593/826 1,000,000 4/15 J.B.C. & A. A.D.S.S./Forms/C. 2118.

Army Form C. 2118

Instructions regarding War Diaries and Intelligence Summaries are contained in F. S. Regs., Part II. and the Staff Manual respectively. Title Pages will be prepared in manuscript.

WAR DIARY
or
INTELLIGENCE SUMMARY
(Erase heading not required.)

Place	Date	Hour	Summary of Events and Information	Remarks and references to Appendices
MERRIS	16th	8.0 am.	Section joined up with other units and marched to CROIX DU BAC, arriving at latter place at 3.30 pm	EJm
CROIX DU BAC	17th	–	Sub-section established at ERQUINGHEM LYS	EJm
CROIX DU BAC and ERQUINGHEM LYS	18, 19th, 20th, 21st, 22nd, 23rd, 24th, 25th, 26th, 27th, 28th, 29th, 30th		Section employed on general sanitary duties including supervision of sanitation of civil and military areas.	EJm

1875 Wt. W593/826 1,000,000 4/15 J.B.C. & A. A.D.S.S./Forms/C. 2118.

S

Oct. 1915

23rd Division

Summarised but not copied

121/7595.

40th Sanitary Section

Vol 2

Oct 15

CONFIDENTIAL

WAR DIARY OF

SANITARY SECTION 40 R.A.M.C(T), 23rd DIVISION

from OCTOBER 1st to OCTOBER 31st 1915

VOLUME II

Instructions regarding War Diaries and Intelligence Summaries are contained in F. S. Regs., Part II. and the Staff Manual respectively. Title Pages will be prepared in manuscript.

WAR DIARY
or
INTELLIGENCE SUMMARY
(Erase heading not required.)

Army Form C. 2118

Place	Date	Hour	Summary of Events and Information	Remarks and references to Appendices
	OCTOBER ~~NOVEMBER~~			
	1st			
	2nd			
	3rd			
CROIX	4th		Section employed on general sanitary duties, including supervision of sanitation of civil and military areas and control of civilians employed on scavenging work.	[illegible]
DU	5th			
BAC	6th			
and	7th			
	8th			
ERQUINGHEM	9th			
LYS.	10th			
(Sub Section)	11th			
	12th			
	13th			
	14th			
	15th			
	16th			
	17th			

1875 Wt. W593/826 1,000,000 4/15 J.B.C. & A. A.D.S.S./Forms/C. 2118.

Instructions regarding War Diaries and Intelligence Summaries are contained in F. S. Regs., Part II. and the Staff Manual respectively. Title Pages will be prepared in manuscript.

WAR DIARY
or
INTELLIGENCE SUMMARY
(Erase heading not required.)

Army Form C. 2118

Place	Date	Hour	Summary of Events and Information	Remarks and references to Appendices
CROIX DU BAC and ERQUINGHEM LYS. (Sub Section)	18th 19th 20th 21st 22nd 23rd 24th 25th 26th 27th 28th 29th 30th 31st		Section employed on general sanitary duties including supervision of sanitation of civil and military areas and control of civilians engaged on scavenging work.	[illegible initials]

1875 Wt. W593/826 1,000,000 4/15 J.B.C. & A. A.D.S.S./Forms/C. 2118.

23rd Division

Summarised but not copied

No: 4 San: Sect.
Vol 3

5

Nov 1915

121
7656

Nov 15

CONFIDENTIAL

WAR DIARY

OF

SANITARY SECTION 40 R.A.M.C.T. 23rd Division

from November 1st to November 30th 1915.

(Volume 4)

Instructions regarding War Diaries and Intelligence Summaries are contained in F. S. Regs., Part II. and the Staff Manual respectively. Title Pages will be prepared in manuscript.

WAR DIARY
or
INTELLIGENCE SUMMARY
(Erase heading not required.)

Army Form C. 2118

Place	Date	Hour	Summary of Events and Information	Remarks and references to Appendices
	NOVEMBER			
CROIX DU BAC. and ERQUINGHEM-LYS. (Sub Section)	1st–18th		Section employed on general sanitary duties including supervision of sanitation of civil and military areas and control of civilians employed on scavenging work.	E.J.Rn.

1875 Wt. W593/826 1,000,000 4/15 J.B.C. & A. A.D.S.S./Forms/C. 2118.

Instructions regarding War Diaries and Intelligence Summaries are contained in F. S. Regs., Part II. and the Staff Manual respectively. Title Pages will be prepared in manuscript.

WAR DIARY
or
INTELLIGENCE SUMMARY
(Erase heading not required.)

Army Form C. 2118.

Place	Date	Hour	Summary of Events and Information	Remarks and references to Appendices
CROIX DU BAC and ERQUINGHEM LYS (Sub Section)	19th, 20th, 21st, 22nd, 23rd, 24th, 25th, 26th, 27th, 28th, 29th, 30th		Section employed on general sanitary duties including supervision of sanitation of civil and military areas and control of civilians employed on scavenging work	EJM

1875 Wt. W593/826 1,000,000 4/15 J.B.C. & A. A.D.S.S./Forms/C. 2118.

23rd Division

S

San: Sect: 40
Vol: 4

Summarised but not copied

121/7911

Dec 1915

CONFIDENTIAL.

WAR DIARY

OF.

SANITARY SECTION 40 RAMCT
23rd Division

from December 1st 1915 to December 31st 1915

(Volume 4).

Instructions regarding War Diaries and Intelligence Summaries are contained in F. S. Regs., Part II. and the Staff Manual respectively. Title Pages will be prepared in manuscript.

WAR DIARY
or
INTELLIGENCE SUMMARY
(Erase heading not required.)

Army Form C. 2118

Place	Date	Hour	Summary of Events and Information	Remarks and references to Appendices
	DECEMBER			
Croix du Bac and Erquinghem (Sub-Section)	1st 2nd 3rd 4th 5th 6th 7th 8th 9th 10th 11th 12th 13th 14th 15th 16th 17th		Section employed on general sanitary duties including supervision of sanitation of civil and military areas and control of civilians employed on ~~scavenging~~ Conservancy work.	[illegible]

1875 Wt. W593/826 1,000,000 4/15 J.B.C. & A. A.D.S.S./Forms/C. 2118.

Instructions regarding War Diaries and Intelligence Summaries are contained in F. S. Regs., Part II. and the Staff Manual respectively. Title Pages will be prepared in manuscript.

Army Form C. 2118

WAR DIARY
or
INTELLIGENCE SUMMARY
(Erase heading not required.)

Place	Date	Hour	Summary of Events and Information	Remarks and references to Appendices
Croix du Bac and Erquinghem	18th 19th 20th 21st 22nd 23rd 24th 25th 26th 27th 28th 29th 30th 31st		Section employed on general sanitary duties including supervision of sanitation of civil and military areas and control of civilians employed on ~~scavenging~~ conservancy work	[illegible]

1875 Wt. W593/826 1,000,000 4/15 J.B.C. & A. A.D.S.S./Forms/C. 2118.

23rd Div.

40th Sany Section

Jan } 1916
Feb } 1916
Mar } 1916
April 1916

CONFIDENTIAL

War Diary of

SANITARY SECTION 40
R.A.M.C. (T) 23rd Division.

from January 1st 1916 to January 31st 1916.

(VOLUME 5).

Instructions regarding War Diaries and Intelligence Summaries are contained in F. S. Regs., Part II. and the Staff Manual respectively. Title Pages will be prepared in manuscript.

WAR DIARY
or
INTELLIGENCE SUMMARY
(Erase heading not required.)

Army Form C. 2118

Place	Date	Hour	Summary of Events and Information	Remarks and references to Appendices
	JANUARY 1916			
Croix du Bac and Erquinghem (Sub Section)	1st, 2nd, 3rd, 4th, 5th, 6th, 7th, 8th, 9th, 10th, 11th, 12th, 13th, 14th, 15th, 16th, 17th, 18th		Section employed on general sanitary duties including supervision of sanitation of civil and military areas and control of civilians employed on conservancy work in the Communes of Steenwerck and Erquinghem Lys.	EJM

1875 Wt. W593/826 1,000,000 4/15 J.B.C. & A. A.D.S.S./Forms/C. 2118.

Instructions regarding War Diaries and Intelligence Summaries are contained in F. S. Regs., Part II. and the Staff Manual respectively. Title Pages will be prepared in manuscript.

WAR DIARY
or
INTELLIGENCE SUMMARY
(Erase heading not required.)

Army Form C. 2118

Place	Date	Hour	Summary of Events and Information	Remarks and references to Appendices
	JANUARY 1916			
Croix du Bac and Erquinghem (Sub Section)	19th, 20th, 21st, 22nd, 23rd, 24th, 25th, 26th, 27th, 28th, 29th, 30th, 31st		Section employed on general sanitary duties including supervision of sanitation of civil and military areas and control of civilians employed on conservancy work in the Communes of Steenwerck and Erquinghem L/S.	[illegible initials]

1875 Wt. W593/826 1,000,000 4/15 J.B.C. & A. A.D.S.S./Forms/C. 2118.

San: Sect: 40

Vol: 6

CONFIDENTIAL

War Diary of Sanitary Section 40 RAMC(T) 23rd Division

from February 1st 1916 to February 29th 1916

(Volume 6)

Instructions regarding War Diaries and Intelligence Summaries are contained in F. S. Regs., Part II. and the Staff Manual respectively. Title Pages will be prepared in manuscript.

WAR DIARY
or
INTELLIGENCE SUMMARY
(Erase heading not required.)

Army Form C. 2118

Place	Date	Hour	Summary of Events and Information	Remarks and references to Appendices
Croix du Bac and Erquinghem L'S (sub section)	FEBRUARY 1st 2nd 3rd 4th 5th 6th 7th 8th 9th 10th 11th 12th 13th 14th 15th 16th 17th 18th 19th 20th		Section employed on general sanitary duties including supervision of sanitation of civil and military areas and control of civilians employed on conservancy work in the Communes of Steenwerck and Erquinghem L'S Instruction etc to men of the 34th Divisional Sanitary Section prior to their taking over the area (Feb. 4th to Feb 11th 1916)	[illegible initials]

1875 Wt. W593/826 1,000,000 4/15 J.B.C. & A. A.D.S.S./Forms/C. 2118.

Instructions regarding War Diaries and Intelligence Summaries are contained in F. S. Regs., Part II. and the Staff Manual respectively. Title Pages will be prepared in manuscript.

WAR DIARY
or
INTELLIGENCE SUMMARY
(Erase heading not required.)

Army Form C. 2118

Place	Date	Hour	Summary of Events and Information	Remarks and references to Appendices
	FEBRUARY			
Croix du Bac and Erquinghem	21st 22nd 23rd		Sub Section from 34th Divisional Sanitary Section arrived to take over work in the area.	
Estaires	24 25		Left Croix du Bac for Estaires – arrived Estaires. Section inspected billets of troops – sanitation found in very bad condition – left for Morbeque.	
Morbeque and Blaringhem	26 27 28 29		Sub Section left at Morbeque – remainder and OC proceeded to Blaringhem. Section left Blaringhem for Camblain Chatelain	[initials]
			Attached is given a detailed account of the duties and work of the Sanitary Section introducing criticism, description and suggestions, for the past six months	

1875 Wt. W593/826 1,000,000 4/15 J.B.C. & A. A.D.S.S./Forms/C. 2118.

Having now left the area which the division has occupied from September 1915 to February 1916, I will append a few notes on the work of the Sanitary Section, during that period, whilst it is still fresh in my mind. The sanitation of a division naturally depends largely on the keenness of the Units comprising it, and I found that some units were very enthusiastic in sanitation work whilst others were the reverse. Whilst speaking of this I would add that I am of opinion that the sanitation and cleanliness of an units encampment rests with the Officer Commanding, the Medical Officer and the senior N.C.O's. The M.O. is however in rather an invidious position for after all he has to keep in with his officers of the unit. Latrines in use were mainly of three different types, but ~~also~~ occassionally long, and short trench latrines. An oil or similiar drum with a perforated bottom standing upon a wooden trough or ash bed, which leads to a soak away pit, the single pail, and the double-tin systems. The first and last were found to be the best, inasmuch as by these methods the urine was either drained away or separated from the fecaies. Thus making it more or less an easier matter for incineration. Thus saving the handling of possible infective material. Whereas the double-tin system does not do this, and incidentally it was found that both tins were fouled with excreta. In a great many instances the latrines were found to be in a very bad condition for with the exception of a few camps, they were without cover, and no attempt had been made to provide comfort for the men. It was not until a week or so before the division left the area, that the Royal Engineers commenced the erection of latrines in the various encampments and had this been done when the troops first

first occupied the area much discomfort would have been saved and latrines kept in a more sanitary condition. It must be generally borne in mind that infantry camps are those chiefly discussed.

The existing urinals were found to be of a very crude description and the ground near them often in a filthy mess owing to the tins, etc., being placed too near the ground. This was however somewhat remedied by the Sanitary Section providing urinals constructed of three tins, one on top of the other, with perforated bottoms — the lower tin being fixed in the ground and the urine thus drained away into a properly constructed urine pit.

Water was obtained from various sources, these being a town supply (800 ft. deep well), public pumps, and in some cases private pumps. Generally the water in this part of France is very open to suspicion, and in cases (mostly farms) it was found so bad that it was forbidden to be used for any purpose by the troops. As a rule the pump of the water cart was not used — the reason being that in the majority of cases it had first to be drawn in buckets, and to pump the water from the buckets through the clarifier would have been a laborious and long task, and more than one could expect an ordinary soldier to do. It was found that the matter in suspension which went into the water cart, after about an half an hour's standing was not contained in the water which came through the taps of the cart which was comparatively clear. The present water cart is in need of of improvement, particularly the use of a more satisfactory pump and also the clarifying cylinder having a better attachment to the drum of the cart. Is it possible to evolve a pump which could be contained in the cylinder?

Cooking places were not very satisfactory. The Royal Engineers had erected open sheds for cooking but no ovens had been made and no grease or soakage pits constructed. The sites were in many cases very ill chosen by units - an instance being when it was found that the spot was exactly over where latrines (short trench) had been.

Ablution benches were fixed in a large number of camps but very few units had made arrangements for the efficient carrying away of waste water. Arrangements must be made for the satisfactory drainage of waste water.

Many of the men were billeted in farms, etc., but a considerable proportion were under canvas - huts and bivouacs. During the latter part of the time the Royal Engineers erected huts which although better from a weather resisting point of view, lacked sufficient ventilation and light. Stoves were not provided in every hut.

Incinerators were chiefly of the closed Bee-hive type which proved to be generally satisfactory

satisfactory and were built by the Sanitary Section. An order was in force that all refuse (including excreta) was to be burned, but owing to the weather conditions and the consequent wetting of the refuse, this was not always possible. I know that some refuse was buried, but I believe a very considerable quantity was burned, the ground thus being saved ~~being~~ pollution to a large extent.

The condition of horse lines depended largely on the units. Some of the latter displayed great energy in constructing covered-in horse stands with tree poles and straw roofs.

Manure was largely taken by the farmers, but carts for collecting it having great difficulty in passing over the fields of mud, it was not done altogether satisfactorily. The mud question could I think have been obviated considerably if a little more foresight had been exercised in the laying of brick or other roadways. As it was the fields were at times impassable.

The number of infectious disease cases which occurred in the division was small. The number included one case of diphtheria, one case of Scarlet fever, two cases of paratyphoid and three of Cerebro spinal meningitis. Herewith the table is appended of the cases and suspected cases disinfected by the Sanitary Section. The

The troops were pretty free from vermin on account of the excellent baths provided. These were worked under the officers and men of ~~the~~ any Field Ambulance.

ERYSIPELAS	MEASLES	DIPHTHERIA		SCARLET FEVER	
		POSITIVE	NEGATIVE	POSITIVE	NEGATIVE
1.	5.	1.	4.	1.	2

CERE. SPINAL. MENI.		TYPHOID		PARA-TYPHOID		MUMPS
POSITIVE	NEGATIVE	P.	N.	P.	N.	
3.	3.	1.	3.	1.	1.	1

SUSPECTED CASES NOTIFIED AND DISINFECTION CARRIED OUT. 27.
DIAGNOSIS SUBSEQUENTLY AS POSITIVE ——————— 14

The surrounding areas of camps were not always found clean, the ground sometimes being strewn with refuse and occasionally defaecations of the men. In the infantry units difficulty often arose through units leaving their camps in a dirty condition, little or no effort being made at times to clean out huts, &c., In these more or less permanent camps I think that each camp ought to have a permanent sanitary fatigue.

Generally speaking, one must use immense tact when dealing with the civil authorities but at times even this does not suffice. It appears to be generally accepted by the people that as the British Army is occupying the area, they, the civil authorities, are relieved of all responsibility, particularly financially. I found this applied especially to Sanitary work, and in the case of the Commune of Steenwerck very little assistance was given - if anything, they

they obstructed the work. Altogether 30 Civilians were employed by the Sanitary Section, in cleaning the roads and the collecting & burning of refuse; 16 in Erquinghem, 6 in Steenwerck and 8 in the villages of Croix du Bac. The cost of employing these Civilians was borne entirely by the British Authorities.
The Communes supplied the carts, and the Field Ambulance the team labour.

SANITARY SECTION
No.
Date
2[illegible] DIVISION

A few notes on the organisation of the Sanitary Section under my command though naturally a hard and fast rule cannot be laid down since each divisional area varies from another in many points for instance of town or country etc. The particular district I am describing was resolved into 3 main areas and 10 subsidiary areas because there happened to be two small townships and a village which consequently permitted of this arrangement. It was found necessary owing to the large area covered by the division, to split the Section into two parts, one of which remained near the Headquarters and the other part billeted in one of the small towns. Each main area was placed under a senior NCO who had three or more men put under his charge. Reports were handed in each day by the men inspecting to their NCO in charge and if any unit was not carrying out it's sanitary work satisfactorily the attention of the OC was drawn to it and he took such action as he thought necessary.

The conservancy work of the communes was supervised by the Section and the method of carrying out the work was that civilians were employed for the purpose and paid by the Sanitary Section, carts being supplied by the communes and the team labour provided by the Field Ambulances. As I am only discussing organisation I do not think it is necessary to describe in detail this work.

I append a table showing how each NCO and man of the Section was more or less employed.—

Sanitary Section Headquarters

O C
Staff Sergt . . . . Acted as Q M S etc
1 L/c Corporal . . . . Clerk
1 L/c Corporal . . . . Supervision of horse brands [illegible] and odd work
1 Private . . . . Batman
1 . . . . Cook
1 . . . . Messenger and odd work
2 A S C Privates . . . . . Lorry drivers

Main Area No I

L/c Sergt . . . . In charge of district
1 Private (No 10 sub area) Supervision of village conservancy works, cookhouses and [illegible] and
1 (No 7) inspecting billets
1 (No 8)
1 (No 9)

Main Area No II

Acting Corporal . . . . In charge of district
1 L/c Corporal (No 5 sub area) Inspecting billets
1 Private (No 6 sub area) Supervision of village conservancy work and cookhouses
1 Private (No 7 sub area) Inspecting billets

Main Area No III

Sergt . . . . In charge of district
L/c Sergt . . . . In charge of conservancy work and cookhouses
L/c Cpl (No 1 sub area) Inspecting billets
L/c Cpl (No 4 sub area)
1 Pte (No 2 sub area)
1 Pte (No 3 sub area)
1 Pte . . . Cook
1 Pte [illegible]

It will be noted that the corporals have been promoted to lance sergeants and the lance corporal to acting corporal and five privates to acting lance corporals. The NCO's and men were paid fortnightly and a kit inspection took place about once a month. The motor lorry was sent into the workshops once monthly for overhauling.

The usual daily routine was as follows –

Reveillé	6–30 am
Breakfast	7–15 am
Parade for duties	8 – 0 am
Dinner	5 – 0 pm
Parade for orders	9 – 0 pm
Lights Out	9–30 pm
to Special orders	

As some of the camps were several miles away it was found more convenient for the men to have dinner at the end of the days work rather than at mid day. The arrangements as described in the foregoing have been found to work satisfactorily and generally speaking units received visits in some cases daily and in others once to twice a week.

40 San Sec
Vol 7

CONFIDENTIAL.

WAR DIARY OF

SANITARY SECTION 40 R.A.M.C.(T) 23rd DIVISION

from March 1st to March 31st 1916.

(Volume ~~8~~ 4)

Instructions regarding War Diaries and Intelligence Summaries are contained in F. S. Regs., Part II. and the Staff Manual respectively. Title Pages will be prepared in manuscript.

WAR DIARY
or
INTELLIGENCE SUMMARY
(Erase heading not required.)

Army Form C. 2118

Place	Date	Hour	Summary of Events and Information	Remarks and references to Appendices
	MARCH			
	1st	–	Inspection of new area commenced. Sub Section posted at BRUAY.	
	2nd	–	Investigation of water supplies and infectious disease cases at CAMBLAIN - CHATELAIN. Cases of typhoid found and houses placed "Out of Bounds". Several pumps marked "Not to be used by the troops".	
	3rd	–	Investigation of water supply and infectious disease cases at PERNES. Nothing of serious importance found.	
	4th 5th 6th	–	Section employed in camp inspection and testing water supplies.	E.J.M.
	7th	–	Sub Section returned to Camblain Chatelain.	
	8th	–	Section proceeded to GRAND SERVINS and billeted with 70th Field Ambulance.	
	9th 10th	–	Section employed in camp inspection and testing water supplies	
	9th	–	O.C. accompanied D.A.D.M.S to ABLAIN ST. NAZAIRE to inspect water supplies.	
	10th	–	O.C. and one sergeant testing water supplies at ABLAIN ST NAZAIRE	

1875 Wt. W593/826 1,000,000 4/15 J.B.C. & A. A.D.S.S./Forms/C. 2118.

Army Form C. 2118

Instructions regarding War Diaries and Intelligence Summaries are contained in F. S. Regs., Part II. and the Staff Manual respectively. Title Pages will be prepared in manuscript.

WAR DIARY
or
INTELLIGENCE SUMMARY
(Erase heading not required.)

Place	Date	Hour	Summary of Events and Information	Remarks and references to Appendices
	MARCH			
	11th	–	Section employed in camp inspection and testing water supplies. Headquarters of Section removed to GAUCHIN LEGAL	
	12th 13th 14th 15th	–	Section employed in camp inspection etc. O.C calling at various Mairies for information in regard to infectious cases and water supplies.	
	15th	–	O.C proceeded to SAINS-EN-GOHELLE to meet O.C Sanitary Section 2nd Division in regard to new area.	[initials]
	16th	–	Sub Section joined remainder of Section at GAUCHIN LEGAL and marched to billets at BRUAY. O.C. proceeded to HERSIN and BARLIN in connection with inspection of private laundries.	
	17th 18th 19th 20th 21st		Section employed in camp inspection etc. O.C investigated infectious disease cases amongst civilian population, also military cases. Sergeant and 10 men proceeded to SAINS EN GOHELLE to get in touch with work in new area	

1875 Wt. W593/826 1,000,000 4/15 J.B.C. & A. A.D.S.S./Forms/C. 2118.

Army Form C. 2118

Instructions regarding War Diaries and Intelligence Summaries are contained in F. S. Regs., Part II. and the Staff Manual respectively. Title Pages will be prepared in manuscript.

WAR DIARY
or
INTELLIGENCE SUMMARY
(Erase heading not required.)

Place	Date	Hour	Summary of Events and Information	Remarks and references to Appendices
	MARCH			
	22nd	–	Remainder of Section proceeded to SAINS-EN-GOHELLE.	
	23rd	–	One N.C.O and two men posted at BARLIN, BULLY-GRENAY, AIX-NOULETTE and CITIÉ-CALONNE respectively	
	24th, 25th, 26th, 27th	–	Section employed in supervision of conservancy work in BARLIN, HERSIN, FOSSE 10 and SAINS EN GOHELLE, in conjunction with the various Town Majors, and camp inspection and water testing.	[initials]
	28th, 29th, 30th, 31st	–	O.C. investigated military and civil infectious cases; inspection of sanitary conditions of the various units and visiting and inspecting areas supervised by respective squads of the section.	

1875 Wt. W593/826 1,000,000 4/15 J.B.C. & A. A.D.S.S./Forms/C. 2118.

40 San Sec
Vol 8

CONFIDENTIAL

War Diary of Sanitary Section 40, R.A.M.C.(T) 23rd Division

from 1st April 1916 to 30th April 1916

(Volume 8)

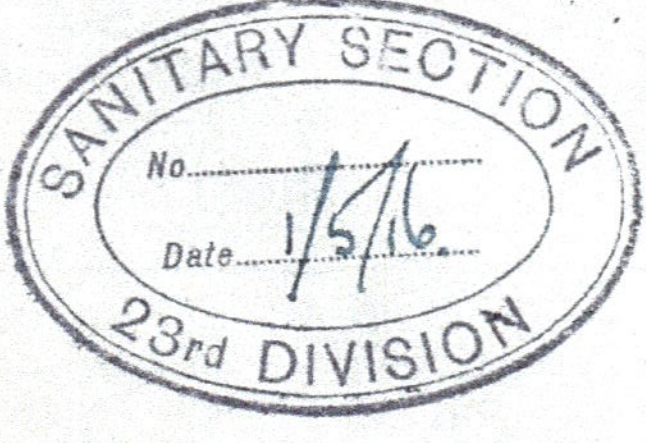

Instructions regarding War Diaries and Intelligence Summaries are contained in F. S. Regs., Part II. and the Staff Manual respectively. Title Pages will be prepared in manuscript.

WAR DIARY
or
INTELLIGENCE SUMMARY
(Erase heading not required.)

Army Form C. 2118

Place	Date	Hour	Summary of Events and Information	Remarks and references to Appendices
Headquarters and main section at SAINS EN GOHELLE Squads at BARLIN, BULLY-GRENAY, AIX-NOULETTE and CITIE-CALONNE	APRIL 1st 2nd 3rd 4th 5th 6th 7th 8th 9th 10th		Section personnel employed in supervision of conservancy work in BARLIN, HERSIN FOSSE 10 and SAINS EN GOHELLE in conjunction with the various Town Majors, camp inspection and periodical testing of water supplies. O.C. investigated military and civil infectious disease cases; inspection of sanitary conditions of the various units; visiting and inspecting areas supervised by respective squads of the section	[illegible initials]
	11th		Arrival of 33 N.C.O's and men from various infantry battalions of the three brigades, attached to Section as permanent fatigue party in lieu of civilian labour (latter unobtainable).	
	12th		Section employed as above.	
	13th 14th		N.C.O and 8 men of fatigue party proceeded to Sanitary Section squad at BULLY GRENAY and 3 men to squad at AIX-NOULETTE	
	15th 16th 17th		Section employed as above. Sub Sections returned from BULLY GRENAY, AIX-NOULETTE and CITIE-CALONNE.	

1875 Wt. W593/826 1,000,000 4/15 J.B.C. & A. A.D.S.S./Forms/C. 2118.

Army Form C. 2118

Instructions regarding War Diaries and Intelligence Summaries are contained in F. S. Regs., Part II. and the Staff Manual respectively. Title Pages will be prepared in manuscript.

WAR DIARY
or
INTELLIGENCE SUMMARY
(Erase heading not required.)

Place	Date	Hour	Summary of Events and Information	Remarks and references to Appendices
	APRIL 18th		Staff Sergt and 9 men proceeded to BRUAY to take over from 2nd Divisional Sanitary Section. Fatigue men of 69th Brigade proceeded on instruction with 69th Brigade for manouvre area.	
BRUAY	19th		Remainder of section marched to BRUAY	
	20th 21st 22nd 23rd		Carrying on with sanitary scheme for town commenced by the 2nd Divisional Sanitary Section. Investigation of military and civil cases of infectious disease, inspection of camps etc. Supervision of conservancy work in conjunction with Town Major	[illegible]
	24th		One N.C.O. and one man posted at DIEVAL.	
	25th 26th 27th 28th 29th		Section employed as above. Fatigue men employed on ~~construction~~ and conservancy work	
	30th		One N.C.O and one man proceeded to manouvre area.	

1875 Wt. W593/826 1,000,000 4/15 J.B.C. & A. A.D.S.S./Forms/C. 2118.

23rd Div

40 San Sec

Vol 9

May 1916

CONFIDENTIAL

WAR DIARY OF SANITARY SECTION 40 R.A.M.C.T.

FROM MAY 1st to MAY 31st 1916

(VOLUME 9)

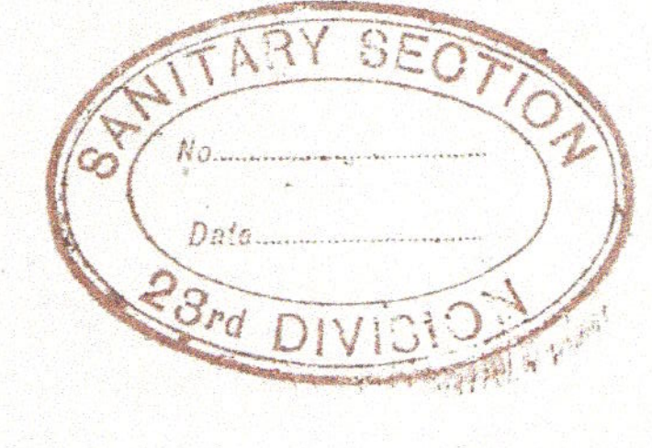

Army Form C. 2118

WAR DIARY
or
INTELLIGENCE SUMMARY
(Erase heading not required.)

Instructions regarding War Diaries and Intelligence Summaries are contained in F. S. Regs., Part II. and the Staff Manual respectively. Title Pages will be prepared in manuscript.

Place	Date	Hour	Summary of Events and Information	Remarks and references to Appendices
	MAY			
BRUAY	1st, 2nd, 3rd	–	Section employed in visiting units encampments and billets for inspection of sanitary arrangements, disinfecting billets in infectious disease cases, periodical testing of water supplies. Carrying on with scheme (commenced by 2nd Division) for sanitation of BRUAY. Attached men employed on conservancy work arranged in conjunction with Town Major and assisting in constructional work. O.C. visited various units with their respective Medical Officers inspecting camps etc. Cookhouses did not appear to be in satisfactory places, in some cases and removal to a more suitable place was suggested. In this connection it may be pointed out that the advice of the Sanitary Officer in the selection of billets would be worth consideration. This suggestion was made to A.D.M.S. and the advantage of Mackenzie disinfecting sprayers being supplied to each Regimental Medical Officer, discussed. A form to be entered up by M.O.'s on the sanitary conditions of encampments when taken over by units, was drafted. This form was approved and ~~taken~~ into use.	
	4th		O.C. directed by Divisional Routine Order to superintend and arrange for the destruction of clothing considered unserviceable by Divisional Board	

1875 Wt. W593/826 1,000,000 4/15 J.B.C. & A. A.D.S.S./Forms/C. 2118.

Army Form C. 2118

Instructions regarding War Diaries and Intelligence Summaries are contained in F. S. Regs., Part II. and the Staff Manual respectively. Title Pages will be prepared in manuscript.

WAR DIARY
or
INTELLIGENCE SUMMARY
(Erase heading not required.)

Place	Date	Hour	Summary of Events and Information	Remarks and references to Appendices
	MAY			
	5th	–	Continuation of work as in previous days. Investigations of both civil and military infectious disease cases. Experiment to be made with new	
	6th	–	disinfectant "C" Solution, but supply not arrived.	
	7th	–	Instructed to confer with O.C. Sanitary Section 2nd Division regarding C. Solution. Saw O.C. 2nd Dvl San. Sec. – solution to be used with syringes.	
BRUAY			Review of work etc with Capt. Mackintyre RAMC who is to act as O.C. Section whilst I am on leave.	
	8th	–	O.C. proceeded on leave to England.	
	9th	–	Capt. Mackintyre acting O.C.	[illegible]
	10th	–	30 gallons C Solution drawn. Weather wet and unsuitable for solution to be used. Journey to O.C. Sanitary Section 2nd Division in regard to scheme for dumping manure in specified dumps in order that it might more easily be treated for flies etc.	
	11th	–	Sub Sections recalled from Manoeuvre Area and from BAJUS and DIVION. Investigation by acting O.C. of infectious disease (military) case at BEUGIN. Advanced party sent to SAINS EN GOHELLE to take over from 2nd Division	
	12th	–	Completion of Sanitation scheme for BRUAY.	
	13th	–	Remainder of Section moved to SAINS EN GOHELLE	

1875 Wt. W593/826 1,000,000 4/15 J.B.C. & A. A.D.S.S./Forms/C. 2118.

Army Form C. 2118

Instructions regarding War Diaries and Intelligence Summaries are contained in F. S. Regs., Part II. and the Staff Manual respectively. Title Pages will be prepared in manuscript.

WAR DIARY
or
INTELLIGENCE SUMMARY
(Erase heading not required.)

Place	Date	Hour	Summary of Events and Information	Remarks and references to Appendices
	MAY 14th	—	Sub Section of Sanitary Section personnel and attached men posted at BULLY-GRENAY AIX NOULETTE and BARLIN.	
SAINS EN GOHELLE, BULLY GRENAY, AIX NOULETTE	15th	—	Investigation of official sources of water supply in all parts of Divisional area including the trenches. Chart and sketch map prepared, showing sources, description of supply and method of drawing water. Following up infectious cases, special attention being paid to the sanitary arrangements existing at COUPIGNY hut encampment where several infectious cases had occurred	[illegible]
HERSIN	16th	—	Conservancy scheme prepared for SAINS EN GOHELLE.	
BARLIN	17th	—	acting O.C. proceeded on leave to England.	
	18th	—		
	19th	8-30am to 12pm.	O.C. returned from leave. List of water carts & personnel ~~to be~~ prepared. Regimental water personnel to be tested by Sanitary Section in their knowledge of sterilisation and condition of all water carts to be obtained. Difficulty experienced regarding the water for small units which have no water cart and no receptacle for holding sufficient quantity of water for sterilisation. Sanitary arrangements and water for trenches to be supervised by Sanitary Section.	
	20th	9am to 10pm	Weather sunny and warm. Interview with ~~O.C. [illegible] Field Coy~~ acting C.R.E. ~~Aix Noulette~~ in regard to water for the trenches. Obtained five brass syringes from D.D.M.S. IV Corps	

1875 Wt. W593/826 1,000,000 4/15 J.B.C. & A. A.D.S.S./Forms/C. 2118.

Army Form C. 2118

Instructions regarding War Diaries and Intelligence Summaries are contained in F. S. Regs., Part II. and the Staff Manual respectively. Title Pages will be prepared in manuscript.

WAR DIARY
or
INTELLIGENCE SUMMARY
(Erase heading not required.)

Place	Date	Hour	Summary of Events and Information	Remarks and references to Appendices
			for use with C. Solution which is on late instructions to be used diluted 1 in 20 and not undiluted. All latrines to be of deep covered pit pattern – model one constructed in Park at SAINS EN GOHELLE by Sanitary Section. Further list to be prepared of water supplies in consequence of Division changing front line.	
SAINS EN GOHELLE, BULLY GRENAY, AIX NOULETTE, HERSIN, BARLIN.	21st	7-45 am to 10-45 pm	Weather fine and warm. C. Solution applied to small quantities of manure, carcases of rats etc as experiment. Comparison to be made between treated and untreated manure and treated and untreated carcases. Section employed on inspection of billets, building incinerators, investigation and disinfection in infectious disease cases. Attached men employed on conservancy work.	[initials]
	22nd	8-0 am to 11 pm	Continuing with experiment on C. Solution. Investigation of water supply for COUPIGNY Huts, VERDREL and BOUVIGNY WOODS	
	23rd	7-45 am to 10-30 pm	Tests with C. Solution finished. ~~Solution good as deodorant, ... but not good as a germicide~~. No harmful effect upon hands of operators if vaseline ~~before~~ be applied before use, to hands and arms.	
	24th	8-0 am to 9-30 pm	Shelling by enemy of SAINS EN GOHELLE – Compelled to take cover for a time. Reported on C. Solution. Brass syringes to A.D.M.S.	

1875 Wt. W593/826 1,000,000 4/15 J.B.C. & A. A.D.S.S./Forms/C. 2118.

Army Form C. 2118

Instructions regarding War Diaries and Intelligence Summaries are contained in F. S. Regs., Part II. and the Staff Manual respectively. Title Pages will be prepared in manuscript.

WAR DIARY
or
INTELLIGENCE SUMMARY
(Erase heading not required.)

Place	Date	Hour	Summary of Events and Information	Remarks and references to Appendices
	MAY			
	25th	8-0 am to 10 pm	Report to be prepared on effects of excess of solder in messtins and camp kettles – what proportion of tins and kettles showed excess of soldering	
SAINS-EN-GOHELLE	26th		Inspection of water supplies & latrines in trenches. Information obtained regarding source of supply. SAINS EN GOHELLE shelled in afternoon – took cover in C.R.E.'s office.	
BULLY GRENAY				
AIX NOULETTE				
HERSIN	27th	4-50 am to 10 pm	Arranged for 9th S. Staffords to build Horsfall destructor at HERSIN	
BARLIN			Visited trenches – Angres sector.	
	28th	–	Visited sub-section at BULLY GRENAY – inspections with Sanitary Section N.C.O. there. Visited Boyeffles & BOUVIGNY. 1 N.C.O. and 10 men reported for duty as fatigue party from 69th Brigade	[illegible]
	29th	–	Inspection of units in various areas – SAINS-EN-GOHELLE shelled by enemy. Instructed at close of shelling for Office and Headquarter staff to proceed to billets at BARLIN – arrived at BARLIN. Attached men and large proportion of section left in advanced areas.	
BARLIN				
	30th	–	Inspecting units etc in different parts of Divisional Area.	
	31st	–	Investigation of messtins at some units for preparation of report.	

1875 Wt. W593/826 1,000,000 4/15 J.B.C. & A. A.D.S.S./Forms/C. 2118.

June 1916

NO 40 San Sec
Vol 10
June

CONFIDENTIAL

WAR DIARY OF

Sanitary Section 40 R.A.M.C.T. 23rd Division
from June 1st 1916 to June 30th 1916
(Volume 10)

Instructions regarding War Diaries and Intelligence Summaries are contained in F. S. Regs., Part II. and the Staff Manual respectively. Title Pages will be prepared in manuscript.

WAR DIARY
or
~~INTELLIGENCE~~ SUMMARY
(Erase heading not required.)

Army Form C. 2118

Place	Date	Hour	Summary of Events and Information	Remarks and references to Appendices
BARLN	1-6-16	–	Ptes Dake & Beresford before me on charge of drinking in billet during prohibited hours. Award [illegible]. About 9.30 am to see ADMS. [illegible] mentioned one or two small matters & then [illegible] instructions to inspect D.A.C. camp.	
		10.30 am	Proceeded to D.A.C. camp & carried out a thorough inspection. In regard to huts I found as in other camps that the middle of the floor was well swept but that the [illegible] under the beds & boards men slept on that practically nothing is done. Called attention to it. Advised to remove one of the cooking places which was not in a very sanitary spot. Also saw an ASC Officer 2nd Div. unit & pointed out a pit being used by his men in which refuse had been ~~thrown~~ & a considerable number of flies on the material. Informed him the refuse should all be burned. Returned about 1.15 pm	[illegible initials]
		1.15 pm	Went [illegible] units with Sergt Ellis [illegible] & inspected mess tins & camp kettles.	
		2.0 to 4.45	Called at Ordnance to see if I could get any information but could not glean any information. Visited 23rd Sqdn RE. Ordnance Men. 340 MT ASC. 190 Co ASC 192 Co ASC. Attached men ASC MVC. & Workshops A.S.C. Find it very difficult to decide what is [illegible] [illegible] in [illegible] of soldiers which are to be used.	
		5.0	Proceeded to [illegible] [illegible] conference at Gas School. Spoke to some of the NCOs re mess tins etc. Opinions varied somewhat. Called at Byffles to see Sergt [illegible] if anything to report	
		4.30	At office to hear reports of NCOs. To dinner	
		9.0	Called in office.	

1875 Wt. W593/826 1,000,000 4/15 J.B.C. & A. A.D.S.S./Forms/C. 2118.

Instructions regarding War Diaries and Intelligence Summaries are contained in F. S. Regs., Part II. and the Staff Manual respectively. Title Pages will be prepared in manuscript.

~~WAR~~ Diary DIARY
or
~~INTELLIGENCE SUMMARY~~

(*Erase heading not required.*)

Army Form C. 2118

Place	Date	Hour	Summary of Events and Information	Remarks and references to Appendices
	2.6.16	8 AM	To office censoring letters &c.	
		9 AM	To see ADMS discussed re solder report in view of impending telegram.	
			With Sgt Elkington I inspected units in regard to excess solder, units visited in the morning being 70th F.A. 9th Yorks 8th Yorks ~~10th W Riding~~ and one of Ford A. Cars	
		1.30	Lunch	
		2.0	Visited 10th W. Riding, 11th NF & 23rd Div Tunnelling Co. Intended visiting 101st RE but they had moved. In connection with solder report on way called in to [illegible] school [illegible] at	[illegible] Field ambulance
			Found matter of deciding re excess solder as being rather a difficult one. To me it seems investigation of camp kettles &c before issue would give a better idea. ~~[illegible]~~ an expert in soldering i.e. tinsmith &c should examine & state his opinion as to whether less solder could have been used. I will attach a report of my enquiries which I submitted to ADMS but which he told me he considered was not a report but a draft of letter. I disagree entirely.	[initials]
		6.15	Tea	
		6.30	Office work. this consists of a number of small matters difficult to mention.	
		7.30	Dinner	
		9.30	To see ADMS at his request. He only required information re Pte Edwards who had been sent to [illegible] at [illegible]. He wants for a man to fill the vacancy. Pte Edwards belonged 12 DLI	
			Owing to rush of work diary not very full for ~~[illegible]~~ the last two days. This is being written in the ~~[illegible]~~ spare [illegible]	

1875 Wt. W593/826 1,000,000 4/15 J.B.C. & A. A.D.S.S./Forms/C. 2118.

Instructions regarding War Diaries and Intelligence Summaries are contained in F. S. Regs., Part II. and the Staff Manual respectively. Title Pages will be prepared in manuscript.

WAR DIARY
or
INTELLIGENCE SUMMARY
(Erase heading not required.)

Army Form C. 2118

Place	Date	Hour	Summary of Events and Information	Remarks and references to Appendices
Barlin	3/6/16	AM 8.10	To office from [illegible] my papers. Instructed Sergt Ellington to investigate re a case of suspected enteric at Company Huts, as on reference I find a previous case had been evacuated a ~~week~~ months before. Received a note last night from ADMS re sanitation of a cavalry detachment encamped in Rudel Wood, also two other matters contained in note [illegible] ~~alt~~ alterations to latrines Company Huts & advice required by M.O 9th Yorks. Having previously made up my mind to visit trenches I decided to instruct Sergt Ellington to get matter of latrine alteration under way. I proceeded	
		10.0	to [illegible] by bicycle & walked with Sergt Chapman to Aix Noulette. On the way met an M.O (i/c 2nd Heavy [illegible]) who is attached at [illegible] [illegible] spoke highly of "C" solution & asked if some could be obtained for use — M.O. [illegible]. Inspected latrines of A.D.S. Two in use. Saw Capt [illegible] & said I would try to get him some incinerator latrine pails. These were	EJ [illegible]
		11.30	used in the [illegible] & flies were practically absent. Borrowed steel helmet & started for ~~trenches~~ with L/Cpl [illegible]. Inspected water supply which is situated along trench. Found M.O. i/c 13th D.L.I. Capt [illegible] he was acting for Capt Shaw on leave. M.O inspected 5 latrines one in front line. Had discussion about labour for digging latrines with adjutant who said ~~[illegible]~~ there was not available men for the work by work	

1875 Wt. W593/826 1,000,000 4/15 J.B.C. & A. A.D.S.S./Forms/C. 2118.

Instructions regarding War Diaries and Intelligence Summaries are contained in F. S. Regs., Part II. and the Staff Manual respectively. Title Pages will be prepared in manuscript.

WAR DIARY
or
INTELLIGENCE SUMMARY
(Erase heading not required.)

Army Form C. 2118

Place	Date	Hour	Summary of Events and Information	Remarks and references to Appendices
	3/6/16		was to be done would take ADMS to read orders. A shell came over one both went first in mess room other in deep dug out. There is no doubt that great difficulty is experienced by units in carrying out deep pits, problems being (1) labour (2) material (3) conveyance [illegible] (4) amount of work. After shelling ceased I returned to [illegible] & subsequently inspected water supply at RE yard & pump in wood. The latter appears	
		pm	to have little protection from possible contamination though the stream was always flowing. ~~Shall report~~ Decided to report to ADMS	
		4.30	Commenced to return to B[illegible] after, overtaken by O.C. 70th F.A. in a car who gave me a lift, bringing me on to B[illegible].	EJm
		5.15	At office [illegible] through papers & for something to eat at 5.45	
		6.30	Returned to [illegible] orders &c. The amount of work to be done & what appears to me requires to be done personally by a Sen. M.O. [illegible] is enormous & since returning from leave I have practically had not a moment to myself.	
		8.30	Went for dinner. [illegible] came in	
		9.30	Left to report at office of ADMS. He gave me his attention about 10 o'clock.	

1875 Wt. W593/826 1,000,000 4/15 J.B.C. & A. A.D.S.S./Forms/C. 2118.

Instructions regarding War Diaries and Intelligence Summaries are contained in F. S. Regs., Part II. and the Staff Manual respectively. Title Pages will be prepared in manuscript.

WAR DIARY

or

~~INTELLIGENCE SUMMARY~~

(Erase heading not required.)

Army Form C. 2118

Place	Date	Hour	Summary of Events and Information	Remarks and references to Appendices
	3/6/16	10 pm	& discussing my report on "soldering" enquiry, remarked my report was a chatty letter not a report. I find it very hard to give satisfaction to him. In a little discussion on "sanitary section" work he stated that in future it should be of a [illegible] nature & that information should be gathered for future use. I agree with this up to a certain point but I think frequent inspection of billets, camps & investigation of water supply, infectious diseases is equally important. For the time being my mental condition is a little upset & letters do not seem able to think clearly.	
			Left ADMS about 11.30 pm returned to my billet & worked up part of the days diary	
		12.45 am	till 12.45 am.	
	4/6/16 Sunday	am. 8.30	Proceeded to office & censored men's letters. Returned to billet 9.0 for breakfast.	
		9.15	Commenced preparing report on excess solder in meat tins.	
		10.0	Proceeded to D.A.C. to arrange about a horse burial. Saw Adjutant who said spot chosen by Sergt was now out of his area. He pointed out another site which appeared satisfactory from sanitary point.	
		11.0	To see Camp Commandant re verbal complaint from Smith [illegible] [illegible] [illegible] [illegible] Lieut Elkin to make necessary arrangements.	
		11.45	Go on with report as above. Entering notes &c.	
		1.30	Lunch	
		2.0	Completed my report. Time taken on report seems long but it was necessary to get out my notes &c.	
		3.30		

1875 Wt. W593/826 1,000,000 4/15 J.B.C. & A. A.D.S.S./Forms/C. 2118.

Instructions regarding War Diaries and Intelligence Summaries are contained in F. S. Regs., Part II. and the Staff Manual respectively. Title Pages will be prepared in manuscript.

WAR DIARY
or
~~INTELLIGENCE SUMMARY~~
(Erase heading not required.)

Army Form C. 2118

Place	Date	Hour	Summary of Events and Information	Remarks and references to Appendices
	4/6/16	4.0	To see new offices suggested [illegible]. Decided to take them over.	
		4.30	To D.S.C. to see Bayley to borrow some money to pay Pte Shuldrick about to proceed on leave.	
		6.0	Returned to new offices. Reading reports clearing up papers &c.	
		4.30	To billet. Entering up diary.	
		8.0	Dinner	
		9.15	To office for report on excess soldiers in mess tins [illegible] to ADMS. Consulted with Lt Bramwell & an M.O. [illegible] Bn. ADMS said I would go [illegible] report to him.	[illegible]
		10.15	Called at office [illegible] wrote letter to CRE for [illegible].	
		10.30	Am now completing diary for to day	
	5.6.16	am 8.30	To office. Censored letters & cleared up various papers. Instructed interpreter to get certificates of 'no damage'. Saw Col. [illegible] had chat with him. To Field Cashier & drew 450 for men & 125 for Off. Spoke C. Commandant to ask for an AF 3125 for Pte Berry but he did not have a copy nor did he know of a regulation re leave. Saw Ady. ASC, had discussion re various matters.	
		11.15	Rounded to [illegible] in [illegible]. M.O. [illegible] not [illegible] two [illegible] to [illegible] digging party. MO [illegible] came [illegible] camp. Pte Gunner was in charge of [illegible] of [illegible], the 2nd [illegible] requires improving. Officers latrines required. The water supply [illegible]	

1875 Wt. W593/826 1,000,000 4/15 J.B.C. & A. A.D.S.S./Forms/C. 2118.

Instructions regarding War Diaries and Intelligence Summaries are contained in F. S. Regs., Part II. and the Staff Manual respectively. Title Pages will be prepared in manuscript.

WAR DIARY
or
INTELLIGENCE SUMMARY
(Erase heading not required.)

Army Form C. 2118

Place	Date	Hour	Summary of Events and Information	Remarks and references to Appendices
	5.6.16.		unsatisfactory, drawing it from village. Water cart [illegible] daily and advised immediately obtaining [illegible] in some small tanks there (to be put in a G S Waggon) from Company. Incinerators require construction say one large one. Inspection revealed a large amount of food tins, litter &c, improperly disposed of. I [illegible] [illegible] holes & in the woods, and [illegible] not find any [illegible] about. Suggested present latrines (or open trenches &c) be immediately filled	
		1.40	Returned to lunch	
		2.15	To office. Saw S Staff man re Horsfall incinerators. One at [illegible] should be completed to-morrow, they work in 8 hours shifts.	
		2.40	Left to see M.O. 9th Yorks. Could [illegible] inspected latrines. The present arrangement of [illegible] not very satisfactory, [illegible] & box system [illegible] [illegible]. Suggested [illegible] as follows. Found old accumulation of debris under beds of huts. Inspected [illegible] [illegible] [illegible] arrangements. Suggested [illegible] from [illegible] should not be put down [illegible] [illegible] [illegible] arrange [illegible] [illegible]. [illegible] one of the Co Commanders suggested [illegible] cleaning up under the beds in [illegible]. [illegible] [illegible] latrine alterations in progress. Points noted in camp. (1) [illegible] [illegible] [illegible] more or less in [illegible] of [illegible] latrines (2) accumulation of debris under bed floor, (3) Men were taking [illegible] for [illegible] from [illegible]. Inspected camp with [illegible] [illegible] suggested [illegible] be spread [illegible] [illegible] of [illegible] latrines. [illegible] [illegible] be cleaned [illegible] [illegible] of the [illegible] [illegible] [illegible] incinerator one for [illegible] time for [illegible] refuse. M.O. [illegible] [illegible] [illegible] Adjutant re (1) (2) (3).	2 TINS / STRAW ASHES / ASHES / EARTH / BURNT TINS / 3'x1'x2'6" / 2'6"x12"x12" / [illegible initials]
		5.40	Returned to [illegible]	
		6.15	To office, reports from 9th & 4 [illegible] [illegible] & [illegible]. Orders, correspondence &c	
		8.30		

Instructions regarding War Diaries and Intelligence Summaries are contained in F. S. Regs., Part II. and the Staff Manual respectively. Title Pages will be prepared in manuscript.

WAR DIARY
or
INTELLIGENCE SUMMARY
(Erase heading not required.)

Army Form C. 2118

Place	Date	Hour	Summary of Events and Information	Remarks and references to Appendices
BARLIN	5/4/16	pm 9.30	To ADMS Office. Sat [illegible] [illegible] line. Spoke re [illegible] to [illegible] cavalry party & 9th [illegible] & also [illegible] in progress [illegible] [illegible]. [illegible] approved [illegible] table [illegible]. [illegible] [illegible] [illegible] [illegible] [illegible] [illegible]. C. Commandant [illegible] [illegible] [illegible] [illegible] [illegible] [illegible] [illegible]	EJ[illegible]
		11.0	[illegible] morning. Verbal instructions to move.	
	6/4/16	AM 4.30	Instructions to Sgt. Elly [illegible] [illegible] morning, [illegible] up [illegible]	
		8.30	Breakfast	
BOYEFFLES		8.45	To lorry to [illegible] to Boyeffles for billets. On return called [illegible] Tunnelling Co for the purpose of [illegible] a pump for emptying [illegible] cesspool at [illegible] Hospital 41 F.A. Instructions to [illegible] re billeting. To see T. Major at his request. To inspect	EJ[illegible]
		1.0	Anson Battn. with M.O. commenced [illegible] [illegible] 12.30.	
		1.45	To [illegible] M.O. Anson Battn. Inspected [illegible]. Advised re [illegible] [illegible] [illegible]. [illegible] latrines partly [illegible] also [illegible] – [illegible] [illegible] [illegible] being kept in [illegible] condition. There is a difficulty in regard to some billets because they are not in continuous occupation [illegible] if anything is [illegible] it would more or less be [illegible] by the [illegible] of time between occupations. Returned to office at [illegible] [illegible] as far as [illegible]. [illegible] visited 2nd Battn. R.M.L.I. with M.O. inspected billets in [illegible] although [illegible] were [illegible] [illegible] they were undoubtedly in a dirty condition, lack of brooms [illegible] [illegible] assumed as reason for this condition. Promised loan of brooms. Inspected latrines [illegible] completed [illegible] with [illegible] [illegible] under construction. Advised re percentage [illegible] [illegible] also re [illegible] of good works being [illegible] [illegible], [illegible] chlorinated.	

1875 Wt. W593/826 1,000,000 4/15 J.B.C. & A. A.D.S.S./Forms/C. 2118.

Instructions regarding War Diaries and Intelligence Summaries are contained in F. S. Regs., Part II. and the Staff Manual respectively. Title Pages will be prepared in manuscript.

WAR DIARY
or
~~INTELLIGENCE SUMMARY~~
(Erase heading not required.)

Army Form C. 2118

Place	Date	Hour	Summary of Events and Information	Remarks and references to Appendices
	6/6/15		After 2nd Batt R.M.L.I. Sent for M.O. 1st Batt [illegible] visited latrines in use. There were very unsatisfactory. I promised to help in the matter [illegible] of [illegible] etc. My impression of the latter M.O. was that he did not pay sufficient attention to sanitation. [illegible] the M.O. the necessity of [illegible] precautions in regard to latrines owing to [illegible] coming from the East.	
		5.45	Returned Mess.	
		6.0	More letters to censor. [illegible] Discussion with Sgt Humphries re necessity of [illegible] out instructions in regard to [illegible] for men. [illegible] with Sgt Chapman. Orders, [illegible] from ADMS office. Received pamphlet on the [illegible] of [illegible] in camps, billets & hospitals.	EJH
		8.20		
		8.30	Dinner [illegible] ADMS office [illegible] did not come [illegible] reported to Capt McIntyre	
		9.30	re visit to Naval Batt [illegible] spoke of [illegible] report re French [illegible] for [illegible] of place of RE advanced dump.	
		10.30	Returned to billet. [illegible]	
	4.6.15	8.45 AM	Instructions to men re work at Company [illegible] etc. Censoring letters. [illegible] inspected various areas [illegible] attention of Sgt Humphries. [illegible] visited from 10. Great improvement in cleanliness noticeable. To see ADMS in evening [illegible] was annoyed with the matter of sanitation at Gully ADS.	EJH
		10.0 PM		

1875 Wt. W593/826 1,000,000 4/15 J.B.C. & A. A.D.S.S./Forms/C. 2118.

Instructions regarding War Diaries and Intelligence Summaries are contained in F. S. Regs., Part II. and the Staff Manual respectively. Title Pages will be prepared in manuscript.

WAR DIARY
or
INTELLIGENCE SUMMARY
(Erase heading not required.)

Army Form C. 2118

Place	Date	Hour	Summary of Events and Information	Remarks and references to Appendices
	7.6.15 (Contd)		Notes above for the day practically cover work which was largely routine, owing to pressure of work details are not being given.	[illegible]
	8.6.15	8 am	Breakfast. Arrangements for constructional work to [illegible] & [illegible] for ~~[illegible]~~ ADS	
		9.30	To 69th F A from Col. Walker who lent me car to proceed to [illegible]. At this ADS made detailed inspection of sanitary arrangements & after proceeded to advanced posts with Capt Woodhouse. The sanitary conditions were not good & in accordance with instructions from ADMS I made notes re improvements. It certainly seems that some very elementary details escape the notice of M.O.s. My recommendations are recorded in report to A.D.M.S.	
		PM 2.30	Had some lunch with Woodhouse & proceeded to [illegible] ADS 41st F Ambulance.	
		to 3.0.	With MO i/c made close inspection re sanitation & ~~[illegible]~~ my suggestions are recorded in report to ADMS mentioned above.	
		4.30	Returned in a car to [illegible] to attend weekly conference at which ADMS called on me to make a few observations. Owing to shortness of notice I am afraid my remarks were not of much value. The conference lasted till about 6.30. One MO spoke re terrible smell from dead bodies in [illegible] sector & various disinfectants were mentioned including a solution chloride of lime, [illegible] of [illegible] etc. At the finish the ADMS thought such lines might be tried.	
		7.0.	Proceeded to [illegible] again & went on to inspect sanitary arrangements at advanced posts. It came on to rain hard but I completed inspection.	
		9.30	Returned in car lent by M.O.	
			On return drew up rough notes for report but unable to get same in finished form for ADMS	

1875 Wt. W593/826 1,000,000 4/15 J.B.C. & A. A.D.S.S./Forms/C. 2118.

Instructions regarding War Diaries and Intelligence Summaries are contained in F. S. Regs., Part II. and the Staff Manual respectively. Title Pages will be prepared in manuscript.

WAR DIARY
or
INTELLIGENCE SUMMARY
(Erase heading not required.)

Army Form C. 2118

Place	Date	Hour	Summary of Events and Information	Remarks and references to Appendices
	continued 8.6.16	P.M. 10 30	After hasty dinner set out for [illegible] to see ADMS to report. It was raining hard. Met ADMS coming from office & I told him I was sorry I could not let him have written report & he said let him have it tomorrow. Arrived back at billet about 11.30 pm.	[initials]
	9.6.16	A.M. 8.15	Breakfast. On with report of sanitary inspection & suggestions of A.D.S. Also looking into matter of water cart inspection. Censoring letters &c. All the morning was spent on this work. [illegible] RQMS [illegible] to tell [illegible] [illegible] to return with full kit in lorry for duty here. On his arrival about 1 pm. informed him re [illegible] [illegible] [illegible]. Glanced at book "Tropical [illegible]" [illegible] by ADMS & [illegible] [illegible] cart inspection report	[initials]
		1.35 12.15	Lunch	
		2.15	Cycled to [illegible] to see progress [illegible]. Met RQMS [illegible] [illegible] [illegible] him in regard to [illegible] at advanced posts & [illegible] and disinfection of diphtheria case 2nd [illegible]. Went on to [illegible] & on way inspected new [illegible] at RE Dump. A RQMS said he had seen a dead rat [illegible] brought up from well so I saw Major [illegible] 12th RE & asked him if he could arrange to have a man sent down to inspect water tubes to have a cover fixed over top, which he promised to do. He said a supply would probably be available in a few days which would be satisfactory.	
		5.	Saw MO i/c ADS. [illegible] discussed re [illegible] clothing &c. I promised to send [illegible] [illegible] [illegible] & boxes &c.	
		5.0	Returned to [illegible]	
		5.30	Entering diary, censoring letters &c.	

1875 Wt. W593/826 1,000,000 4/15 J.B.C. & A. A.D.S.S./Forms/C. 2118.

Instructions regarding War Diaries and Intelligence Summaries are contained in F. S. Regs., Part II. and the Staff Manual respectively. Title Pages will be prepared in manuscript.

WAR DIARY
or
INTELLIGENCE SUMMARY
(Erase heading not required.)

Army Form C. 2118

Place	Date	Hour	Summary of Events and Information	Remarks and references to Appendices
	Contd 9.6.16		Staff Sgt Rumley & L/Cpl Gunner reported to duty from leave at 12 noon. Delayed one day at Boulogne for which they produced a pass.	
		P.M. 9.45	To see ADMS & handed him report on sanitary arrangements advanced dressing stations which report he said was quite satisfactory.	E.J.A.
	10.6.16	A.M. 8.15	Breakfast	
		9.45 – 12 noon	On with report of water carts & personnel and found that it would be better for me to verify some of the returns before framing my report. Sgt Ellingham assisted [illegible]	
		12 noon	To see O.C. 69th F.A. & told him inspected water carts & transport [illegible] personnel [illegible] were unsatisfactory so he said I should send in a bad report of the matter as he considered that conditions were very far from satisfactory	
		1.15 to 2.0	Lunch	
			At 2.0 proceeded to inspect various units in Bois de Froissart [illegible] The 2nd Sect of 69th F.A., 2nd Northumb. [illegible] & 69th Machine Gun Co.	E.J.A.
		5.15 to 5.45	Tea	
			On with reports, instructions &c. L/Cpl Tabor reported Sgts Humphries & Chapman [illegible]. Received a wire from 69th Bde [illegible] saying "send back 1 NCO & [illegible] tonight". I sent telegram to the ADMS who saw me about it when I reported at 10 o'clock [illegible] instructed me not to send the men back. [illegible] report [illegible] longer than anticipated, he said I should have more [illegible] in a day or two	

1875 Wt. W593/826 1,000,000 4/15 J.B.C. & A. A.D.S.S./Forms/C. 2118.

Instructions regarding War Diaries and Intelligence Summaries are contained in F. S. Regs., Part II. and the Staff Manual respectively. Title Pages will be prepared in manuscript.

WAR DIARY
or
INTELLIGENCE SUMMARY
(Erase heading not required.)

Army Form C. 2118

Place	Date	Hour	Summary of Events and Information	Remarks and references to Appendices
	contd		ADMS instructed me to be at his office at 10.30 am tomorrow to meet O.C. San Sec 47th Div. In walking to Headqrs ADMS informed me that [illegible] staff officers [illegible] about [illegible]	
	10.6.16		Returned to billet about 10.30 pm with Smith. [illegible] showery all day. [illegible]	[illegible]
	11.6.16	8.15 am	Sgt [illegible] & Cpl Penfold reported for explanation of [illegible] re [illegible] Verdrel Wood. On with diary, notes &c. Car which I asked for yesterday did not arrive till about 11 o'clock, the driver informed me he had gone to [illegible] as he was not told where office was. With him returned to my office. To ADMS office at 10. Met O.C. San Sec 47th Div. & informed him of works in this area in regard to water supply, conservancy scheme at the commune & various dumps, arrangement of rations, &c. He asked for loan of various maps &c which he promised to return if I would leave them with me. He left about 1 pm	
		2.0 pm	With Sgt Elkington in car to 4th F.A. re water carts, also to Company [illegible] had found 47th Div unit in. On to Verdrel [illegible] & [illegible] F.A. [illegible] To 70 F.A. re [illegible] also 192 Co A.S.C., Headqrs, 2 & 3 section D.A.C. & various RFA wagon lines at [illegible] where I found some of the carts had gone to [illegible] positions. The result of water cart inspection was embodied in report but generally speaking particular care of them was not taken, whilst knowledge of the personnel was not good.	[illegible]
		6.15 – 6.30	Tea	
		8.45	Engaged on notes, report &c.	
			Dinner	
		9.15	Further notes &c	
		9.45	To A.D.M.S. who gave me instructions re removal of [illegible] with O.C. San Sec 47th Div. Spoke re ~~water supply~~ [illegible] for RE [illegible] he said I should give information direct as it was more or less of a [illegible] nature	
		10.15	Returned [illegible]	

Instructions regarding War Diaries and Intelligence Summaries are contained in F. S. Regs., Part II. and the Staff Manual respectively. Title Pages will be prepared in manuscript.

WAR DIARY
or
INTELLIGENCE SUMMARY
(Erase heading not required.)

Army Form C. 2118

Place	Date	Hour	Summary of Events and Information	Remarks and references to Appendices
	12.6.15	AM 8.30	Censoring letters &c	
		9.0	Proceeded on foot with Sergt Elkington to Bully [illegible] met [illegible] of 2nd [illegible] & also [illegible] Gilly M.O of same unit. At Bully met Capt [illegible] & proceeded to [illegible] at A.D.S., [illegible] disappointed to find such a poor job made of the [illegible]. Instructed Capt [illegible] to improve it. Then visited various [illegible] at Bully [illegible] Aix Noulette. In Bully met A.D.M.S who [illegible] one of [illegible] visited [illegible] & [illegible] one or two. The chief object of my inspection was [illegible] water carts. The result of inspection is included in my report. About 1 [illegible] we arrived at Aix Noulette [illegible] & [illegible] 2.15 [illegible] Inspected [illegible] besides) carts, kitchens in camps including 11th W. [illegible] at [illegible] Aix Noulette & various R.F.A. units. Returned to office at 5.40	[initials]
		PM 6.0	Saw A.D.M.S who told me I might go to [illegible] to morrow to look for billets. [illegible] said I [illegible] got in touch with the 9th Div [illegible] more [illegible] would have [illegible]. He said I could have use of car	
		6.30 to 8.30	Returned to office On with reports, orders &c.	
		9.0	Dinner	
		10.0	On with diary, &c. Finished work/ Weather [illegible] all day	
	13.6.15	AM 8.30	Clearing up papers &c preparatory to handing over to 24th Div [illegible]	
		9.45	To [illegible] to Camp Commandant's office [illegible] who said office of A.D.M.S [illegible] To [illegible] office [illegible] 2nd [illegible] for work at [illegible] office was out. To see A.D.M.S [illegible] billets [illegible] at Bruay [illegible] a new one at the same time [illegible] up billets for my own	[initials]

1875 Wt. W593/826 1,000,000 4/15 J.B.C. & A. A.D.S.S./Forms/C. 2118.

Instructions regarding War Diaries and Intelligence Summaries are contained in F. S. Regs., Part II. and the Staff Manual respectively. Title Pages will be prepared in manuscript.

WAR DIARY
or
~~INTELLIGENCE SUMMARY~~
(Erase heading not required.)

Army Form C. 2118

Place	Date	Hour	Summary of Events and Information	Remarks and references to Appendices
	Continued 13.6.18		To Bray & after seeing Town Major proceeded to old billets to advise taking over. After a little trouble found a billet for ADMS which after discussion Town Major said I could have	
			To field Ambulance at [illegible] this morning. The [illegible] belonged to 7th Corps.	
			Returned via Bray & saw ADMS for a few minutes. Arrived back at [illegible] at 1.45.	
			~~[illegible]~~ O.C. [illegible] Sanitary Section arrived about 2 o'clock & after seeing me I made arrangements for billeting for them till they took over	[illegible]
			In morning [illegible] ADMS re drawing memorandum but not able enough to find road, as the weather was wet &c. so it was not a successful [illegible]	
			In afternoon clearing up all papers & [illegible] work with O.C. San Sec 40th Div	
			To see ADMS at 6 pm. He ~~[illegible]~~ [illegible] me to arrange to remove San Officer's material	
		P.M. 10.15	In evening completing clearing up. [illegible]	
			In view of San material [illegible] arrangement about only 1 lorry load, so will endeavour to take some material as well as equipment	
	14.6.18	A.M. 8.30	Lorry did not get away till nearly 9 o'clock. [illegible]	[illegible]
		9.0	Inspection (kit) [illegible] of attached men.	
		11.0	[illegible] Sgt. Humphries to march off with attached men to Bray. Handed over to O.C. S.S. 40th Div	
		11.30	Set out on horse for Bray arrived about 12.45 with [illegible] to lunch after calling at office.	
		2.0	To Bray with [illegible] in Ambulance. San. Officer had gone but saw ADMS 40th Div, who said there were no ~~particular~~ sanitary matters he could inform me re area, manure is burnt, short [illegible] latrines used, water supply generally good. On return to my office about 6 pm found ~~[illegible]~~ [illegible] had arrived from San. Off. 40th Div first saying my visit was convenient, second one cancelling it	

1875 Wt. W593/826 1,000,000 4/15 J.B.C. & A. A.D.S.S./Forms/C. 2118.

Instructions regarding War Diaries and Intelligence Summaries are contained in F. S. Regs., Part II. and the Staff Manual respectively. Title Pages will be prepared in manuscript.

WAR DIARY
or
~~INTELLIGENCE SUMMARY~~
(Erase heading not required.)

Army Form C. 2118

Place	Date	Hour	Summary of Events and Information	Remarks and references to Appendices
BRUAY	Contd 14.6.16		During evening fixing up arrangements.	
		9.30 am	To ADMS office when he told me he had no instructions for me & that I could move when I liked.	
			Time was advanced 1 hour in accordance with French decree, 11 pm became midnight.	[illegible]
			Sanitary Section personnel & attached men all arrived at Bruay. [illegible] Walker, Vet: Gas officer Lt Parker joined mess.	
	15.6.16	9.30 a.m.	Diary, making arrangements &c.	
			Supervising fitting up lorry & inspected attached men before they marched off to Amettes the halting place to Bruay.	
			In afternoon kit inspection of personnel. Lecture to them on pamphlet 'The abolition of flies from billets &c' & other sanitary matters. Impressed on men the necessity for proper treatment of horse manure, the protection of food, the cleanliness of cooks, that the [illegible] should be obtained for deep pit covered latrines, the inspection of public carts & other matters.	[illegible]
			The ADMS looked in & made complaint re public latrine. Instructed Staff Sgt to carry out cleansing immediately but on my inspection later found work had not been done & had to instruct Lcpl Chapman to do the work at once. Later Staff Sgt said he misunderstood order. He thought it referred only to [illegible] in Bruis. At 6.30 pm went with Pickering to concert. Returned at 9.30 pm.	
			To see A.D.M.S. who asked if a lorry could be supplied to Baths section at Bruay tomorrow.	
		P.M. 10.0	I made inquiries & promised that they would be given [illegible] ADMS office tomorrow.	
			At 1 pm lorry left with equipment & following: LCpl Fraser, LCpl McGuinness & Baltrade [illegible] men proceed to Bruay to fix up billets.	

1875 Wt. W593/826 1,000,000 4/15 J.B.C. & A. A.D.S.S./Forms/C. 2118.

Instructions regarding War Diaries and Intelligence Summaries are contained in F. S. Regs., Part II. and the Staff Manual respectively. Title Pages will be prepared in manuscript.

WAR DIARY
or
INTELLIGENCE SUMMARY
(Erase heading not required.)

Army Form C. 2118

Place	Date	Hour	Summary of Events and Information	Remarks and references to Appendices
BRUAY	16.6.16	AM 6.30	To see lorry complete loading. Lorry left at 7 am, with Pickering, Sergt Chapman, L/Cpl Bunnet, Pte Perry proceeded on lorry. Inspected billets found one had been left very unsatisfactory. Instructed Staff Sergt to have the room immediately cleared. Section marched off at 7.50 a.m. 162 strong. Pte Smith left behind to clear up billeting certificates, he caught us up at Fups. The men marched very well. The weather was dull & cool & ideal for marching. We arrived at Bomy at 4.10 pm. The distance is from 16 to 18 miles & halts were made every 40 minutes, the rests varying from 5 up to 15 minutes, the halt at Fups was of 1 hour's duration.	E.J.h.
BOMY			On arrival found attached men had arrived & billets had been fixed up after some little difficulty. Instructed Interpreter & Sergt Chapman to proceed to Enquinpalte re civilian diphtheria case. O.C. Salvage asked to join mess for time being. Office fixed up – same building as APM, it appears to be a 'seed' store. Staff Sergt reported 5 or 6 men reporting with sore heels. To see ADMS at 9.30 pm waited till 10.30 pm but he did not come in.	
		PM 11.0	Returned to office & signed orders &c. Weather, dull at first, fine later.	
	14.6.16	AM 8.30	Parade of personnel. Detailed men to visit various camps & other duties. To see ADMS at 9.30 am, but had to report again at 10.15 am. He said I must keep men to fill in & not put them out. On with sorting out papers, preparing & sending boxes to Bruay & others.	E.J.h.

1875 Wt. W593/826 1,000,000 4/15 J.B.C. & A. A.D.S.S./Forms/C. 2118.

WAR DIARY
or
~~INTELLIGENCE SUMMARY~~

(Erase heading not required.)

Army Form C. 2118

Instructions regarding War Diaries and Intelligence Summaries are contained in F. S. Regs., Part II. and the Staff Manual respectively. Title Pages will be prepared in manuscript.

Place	Date	Hour	Summary of Events and Information	Remarks and references to Appendices
	Contd 17.6.16		During morning arranged re gas school material to be dumped for removal, inspected re latrines at C mess & other odd work	
		p.m. 2.15	Parade for kit issue of personnel. Inspected sanitation at Head Qrs Offices, General's Qrs, B & C mess which generally were unsatisfactory. The area round chateau requires much attention & cooks &c do not seem to keep kitchens &c clean	[illegible initials]
			Gas officer Lt Pickering left for his unit to-day. One box stationery sent to dump at B[illegible]	
			Saw Camp Commandant in morning & spoke re condition of head qrs & he agreed to my suggestion that I should send 6 men to clear up.	
		P.M. 10.30	Reported above to ADMS in evening.	
			Saw DADMS about 3 o'clock re his message that he had [illegible] for me. The same related to [illegible]	
			Whittle [illegible]	
	Sunday 18.6.16	a.m. 9.0	Met ADMS who said he was inspecting headquarters.	
			At 10 a.m. set out with Sergt Elkington to see 12th DLI & 24th Bde units as instructed by ADMS. Found 12 DLI had gone out for training also M.O. Saw O.C. "C" Co. inspected his billets which were very satisfactory on the whole. [illegible] obtained from [illegible] at [illegible] mess. [illegible] made complaint to O.C. C Co re state of kitchen surrounding food at Head' mess. [illegible] billets was a certain amount of old straw which I suggested it would be better taken out. (Ricklingham)	[illegible initials]
			On to Vinchy & inspected 68th M.G. Co. which was very unsatisfactory. See report to ADMS. Rounded to Mallingham saw Transport lines of 101 RE. which were also unsatisfactory. Left message at CRE office for M.O. that I would visit again after lunch. Returned to [illegible] at B[illegible] at 1.50 p.m. Left again for CRE office at 2.45. After clearing up one or two office matters	

Instructions regarding War Diaries and Intelligence Summaries are contained in F. S. Regs., Part II. and the Staff Manual respectively. Title Pages will be prepared in manuscript.

WAR DIARY
or
~~INTELLIGENCE SUMMARY~~
(Erase heading not required.)

Army Form C. 2118

Place	Date	Hour	Summary of Events and Information	Remarks and references to Appendices
	contd 18.6.16		Took wrong road [illegible] at [illegible]. Inspected T.M.B. 68th Bde & found things not satisfactory on report to ADMS. To RE to see M.O. Reported condition of 101 Transport [illegible] visited 102 RE which were more satisfactory. He said he had issued instructions that the C.O. & matters were being rectified. Found his [illegible] CRE [illegible] On to [illegible], but M.O. 9th S. Staffs was out. Inspected a few billets [illegible] with Sanitary Corporal. The conditions though needing some improvement were fair. Returned to office at 4.40 pm At office until 8 pm On returning from billet of [illegible] met [illegible] who had been to see [illegible], who had reported sick. To ADMS office to see ADMS. Discussion re [illegible] particularly in regard to [illegible]. He instructed me to write [illegible] M.O. to [illegible]. He asked for [illegible]. Matters re [illegible] took place as to [illegible] possibility of poisoning of supplies. [illegible] being liable to be splashed with mud &c. Also mentioned re [illegible] he said it was being borne in mind.	[initials]
		P.M. 10.0		
	19.6.16	A.M. 8.45	To see [illegible] who seemed a little better. Inspected billets. To office & on with diary reports &c. To inspect camp of 71st F Amb. Found same satisfactory. Advised free use of chloride of lime & also that old straw should be cleared out of billets. To see 9th Yorks billets as per M.O.'s report handed me by ADMS. Battalion was on manoeuvres & M.O. was with it but inspected the billets with Quartermaster. Found conditions much the same as obtaining throughout the area. Returned to office at 1.50 pm. Found memo from ADMS re [illegible] and [illegible] latrines & found same [illegible] at [illegible] station. Reported this to ADMS.	[initials]

Instructions regarding War Diaries and Intelligence Summaries are contained in F. S. Regs., Part II. and the Staff Manual respectively. Title Pages will be prepared in manuscript.

WAR DIARY
or
~~INTELLIGENCE SUMMARY~~

(Erase heading not required.)

Army Form C. 2118

Place	Date	Hour	Summary of Events and Information	Remarks and references to Appendices
	contd 19.6.16		after lunch 2 15 inspected latrines for urinals as just mentioned. Wrote out reports re visit [illegible]	
		PM	this morning of 71 FA HdQrs for ADMS. At Ouy St Jul. & ~~[illegible]~~ Surry	
		3.0	To visit M.O. [illegible] at Ouy St Jul. re officers wounded suspected diphtheria. Disinfection being carried out & houses marked out of bounds. He said he was [illegible] in [illegible] [illegible] recent [illegible] cases. To [illegible] to see DADOS re police badges but he was out; left message with his sergeant. Saw Mr [illegible] [illegible]. Saw M.O. [illegible] & he said ADMS said he was getting through his new [illegible] for his unit. Discussed re sanitation: ~~[illegible]~~ and cleaning out of straw [illegible] of long narrow deep trench latrines. M.O. remarked ~~that~~ since men had been in the [illegible] they had got a few lice. He asked if arrangements could be made ~~[illegible]~~ re baths & I informed him nearest were at [illegible]. On this [illegible] [illegible] where [illegible] [illegible] RFA [illegible] at [illegible]. [illegible] there inspected [illegible]. No permanent personnel & [illegible] not in good condition. Returned at 6 15 pm	EJ [illegible]
		6.30	At office. [illegible] personnel. On report [illegible] carts &c.	
		8.15 / 9.15	[illegible] After dinner completed report [illegible] carts.	
		10.0 am	To see ADMS with report. He took summary but handed back list of units to have their carts [illegible] added. Received instructions re course [illegible] [illegible] personnel.	
	20.6.16	9.0 am	[illegible] letters &c. To see ADMS re programme for water [illegible] course. To [illegible] saw DADOS who promised [illegible] police badges [illegible]. On returned saw M.O. [illegible] & asked for return of diphtheria cases in his unit. [illegible] made enquiries at Ouy St Julien [illegible] re [illegible] [illegible] but [illegible] [illegible] [illegible] were out — [illegible] [illegible] information could be obtained. Returned at 1.15 pm.	EJ [illegible]

1875 Wt. W593/826 1,000,000 4/15 J.B.C. & A. A.D.S.S./Forms/C. 2118.

Instructions regarding War Diaries and Intelligence Summaries are contained in F. S. Regs., Part II. and the Staff Manual respectively. Title Pages will be prepared in manuscript.

Army Form C. 2118

WAR DIARY
or
~~INTELLIGENCE~~ SUMMARY
(Erase heading not required.)

Place	Date	Hour	Summary of Events and Information	Remarks and references to Appendices
	Contd 20.6.16	2.15	At office & preparing lecture for water course [illegible]. Continuing up diary &c until 5.15	
		5.15	Tea.	[illegible]
		6.0	On with notes for lecture after work &c	
		8.15	Dinner	
		9.15	Orders &. To see ADMS who informed me he had [illegible] out re water lecture.	
		10.0	Weather fine	
	21.6.16	a.m. 9.0	[illegible] letters &c. At 9.30 proceeded to 71 F.A. at [illegible] to give water course [illegible] & also to [illegible] in afternoon to 70 F.A. for similar purpose. The impression I have gathered to-day is that lectures are useful in arousing the interest of the men engaged on particular work which is an excellent thing. To-day's lectures were chiefly on water supplies & the use of water cart but only essential matter was given and too much detail or [illegible] to [illegible] details only wearies the men & is not helpful. In the afternoon before the General with his Aide de Camp visited the 70 F.A. to [illegible] on the ribbon [illegible] by one of the men at [illegible]. He made a few enquiries in regard to the water cart. I had tea with the Ambulance Mess. Returned to office at 5.30 p.m. [illegible] notes [illegible]. At 10 p.m. to see ADMS. O.C. [illegible]. Asked to [illegible] ADMS agreed but [illegible] for the present. [illegible]	[illegible]
		p.m. 10.20	~~[illegible]~~ [illegible] to D.D.M.S. Weather fine	
	22.6.16	a.m. 8.45	To see result of [illegible]. [illegible] on next trial. To 69th Field Ambulance & gave first lecture on [illegible] water supply [illegible]. Saw O.C. 69th [illegible]. A.D.M.S. came [illegible] at [illegible] time of lecture. On return saw Capt [illegible] 71st F.A. who said A.D.M.S. had been asking when [illegible] and [illegible]. After talking it over with him I pointed	[illegible]

1875 Wt. W593/826 1,000,000 4/15 J.B.C. & A. A.D.S.S./Forms/C. 2118.

Army Form C. 2118

Instructions regarding War Diaries and Intelligence Summaries are contained in F. S. Regs., Part II. and the Staff Manual respectively. Title Pages will be prepared in manuscript.

WAR DIARY
or
~~INTELLIGENCE SUMMARY~~

(Erase heading not required.)

Place	Date	Hour	Summary of Events and Information	Remarks and references to Appendices
	Continued 22.6.16		out that it was not necessary to have a car any longer in connection with lectures as I needed only a [illegible] Bay for my second lectures. I told him I did not want car in afternoon.	
		P.M.	Car came in afternoon the drivers not having been informed I did not require it. I [illegible] drivers to return	
		2. 0	Went on horse to 71st Field Amb. at [illegible] St Julien & gave 2nd water lecture.	
		5. 30	Attended M.O's conference at B[illegible] & gave a few notes on water [illegible] at instructions of ADMS there was not much discussion afterwards and no questions were asked. One suggestion was that a San. Sec. man should be [illegible] to each unit for water duties. ADMS said it was not practical owing to only 25 men being in San Sec. He also said that [illegible] about one had had sanitary inspection work in private life. I thought that ADMS remarks were not very flattering or reported knowledge & training of the Section.	E.J.M.
		P.M. 10.30	Drew up standing orders for water supply [illegible]. To see ADMS at 10 pm [illegible] till 10.30 pm but he did not come so I left. Handed standing orders to D A D M S	Weather fine.
	23-6-16	A.M. 8. 45	Censoring letters & To 70th Field Amb. on 2nd water lecture. Arrived a little late as lost the way cycling there. Accompanied by Sergt Elkington. In 2nd lecture [illegible] the means of clarifying & sterilizing water & also ran over details of water cart again. In afternoon proceeded to 69th F.A. at [illegible] for second lecture. Owing to very heavy thunderstorm had to terminate lecture about 5 minutes before finishing. Returned to B[illegible] about 6.15 pm. In evening making arrangements for lorry proceeding to new area. Saw ADMS about 10 o'clock & he asked me if all arrangements were made. He also asked if room for small bag [illegible] man.	E.J.M.
		P.M. 11.30	Saw lorry loaded &c. Final instructions to Staff Sergt.	Weather fine at first. Thunderstorm later.
	24.6.16	A.M. 9. 0	Inspection of billets latrines &c at B[illegible]	E.J.M.
		10. 30	Moving off postponed till 10.30 because of rain. Moved off at 10.30 & had very [illegible] marching to station. Halted 4 or 5 hours at [illegible]. Arrived at [illegible] Station at [illegible] [illegible] PTO 128th Co. R.E. on train & obtained our horses.	Weather / Showery at first Fine later.

1875 Wt. W593/826 1,000,000 4/15 J.B.C. & A. A.D.S.S./Forms/C. 2118.

Instructions regarding War Diaries and Intelligence Summaries are contained in F. S. Regs., Part II. and the Staff Manual respectively. Title Pages will be prepared in manuscript.

WAR DIARY
or
~~INTELLIGENCE SUMMARY~~
(Erase heading not required.)

Army Form C. 2118

Place	Date	Hour	Summary of Events and Information	Remarks and references to Appendices
VAUX	25.6.16		Arrived at [illegible] Station about 9.45. [illegible] about 10.0 [illegible] off about 10.30 [illegible] Marched to Vaux. On the way one [illegible] went sick & was sent to hospital. Arrived at Vaux about [illegible]. [illegible] attached men fell out on route [illegible] All reported by the evening except one sent to hospital. Searched for billet for myself with interpreter. Bedroom arranged for by C. Commandant at ADMS [illegible]	[initials]
		P.M. 10.30	Saw ADMS in evening & received instructions re arrangement of San Section [illegible] attached men [illegible] D.R.O. On return [illegible] orders for the morrow. To bed about 11.30 [illegible]. *Weather, fine*	
	26.6.16	A.M. 8.45	To see ~~men~~ personnel [illegible] to [illegible] Camp Commandant's office with [illegible] attached [illegible] sergeant. At stores [illegible] equipment. Attached men [illegible] for D.R.O. On clearing up of [illegible] &c. → 2 Personnel to RO [illegible] Infantry Brigade. In afternoon inspected village with Sgt [illegible]. Found several trench latrines with covers & [illegible] but these were imperfect in some cases as regards being fly proof. [illegible] Inspected water [illegible] Camp Commandant about [illegible] latrines. He agreed to my [illegible]	[initials]
		P.M. 9.45	Saw ADMS in evening & he instructed me further in regard to stretcher drill &c for personnel remaining. *Weather, Showery*	
	27.6.16	A.M. 9.0	Censoring letters. Sgt from 40th F.A. reported for instruction of personnel — stretcher drill &c. To try to find [illegible] but gave up after 11 o'clock. With Capt Bell to Vaux & inspected 11th W. York. There were several covered trench latrines in a more or less satisfactory state. Instructed that one should be filled up. Water carts were in fair condition. As stay may only be temporary, improvements must be [illegible]. Returned with Capt Bell. [illegible] F.A. mentioned [illegible] latrines. In afternoon to see men at stretcher drill. Instructed Sgt Elkington re duties on [illegible] places also re [illegible] to keep eye on [illegible]. To [illegible] with M.O. 8th Yorks inspected billets & latrines. The latter were not satisfactory, no [illegible] water obtained from [illegible]. On return journey lost my way so gave up idea of proceeding to see 9th [illegible].	[initials]
		P.M. 10.0	After [illegible] diary, orders &c. Saw ADMS & he said he wished to inspect [illegible] before it [illegible] area. *Showery*	

1875 Wt. W593/826 1,000,000 4/15 J.B.C. & A. A.D.S.S./Forms/C. 2118.

Instructions regarding War Diaries and Intelligence Summaries are contained in F. S. Regs., Part II. and the Staff Manual respectively. Title Pages will be prepared in manuscript.

WAR DIARY
or
~~INTELLIGENCE SUMMARY~~
(Erase heading not required.)

Army Form C. 2118

Place	Date	Hour	Summary of Events and Information	Remarks and references to Appendices
	28.6.16	AM 9.0	Large amount of correspondence to look through. Sergt Chapman came in [illegible] re suspected typhoid case 1st Dorsets. I instructed him to verify case of Pte Blacow [illegible] Banks. On billeting certificates &c. At lecture by Sgt [illegible] 70th F.A. [illegible] on First Aid. Inspected loading of lorry. A.D.M.S. inspected lorry with Capt Bell but I was not present. Staff Sergt told me he appeared satisfied. In afternoon read [illegible] in [illegible], [illegible] on First Aid &c.	[illegible]
			In evening got out notes on [illegible] sanitation orders for summer campaign.	
		PM 10.15	Saw ADMS who instructed me to visit Bde [illegible] enquiries re supply [illegible], [illegible] & also what bathing arrangements. He also asked that [illegible] [illegible] supplies be [illegible]. [illegible]	
	29.6.16	AM 9.0	Censoring letters. To headqrs to see D.A.D.O.S but he was out. To Ord. dump [illegible] enquiries re issue of [illegible] [illegible]. Drew 350 [illegible] from field [illegible]. At 10.30 proceeded on bicycle accompanied by Staff Sergt to [illegible] saw M.O. [illegible] re clothing [illegible]. On to St. [illegible] & saw Adjutant 8 [illegible] [illegible] M.O. [illegible]. Called at 9th Yorks on return by M.O. was out at parade. Returned to [illegible] for lunch at 1-30. After lunch 2.15 set out for [illegible] saw M.O. 9th Yorks. At [illegible] saw O.C. T.M.B. 68th Bde who spoke of my report. To Picquigny saw [illegible] 10th N.F. Adj 13th D.L.I. & M.O.s of 12 D.L.I. & 11 N.F. Had cup of tea with M.O. 12 D.L.I. Saw T. [illegible] & told him to see some [illegible] [illegible] by a former division. Saw Capt Hutchinson [illegible] who explained re sanitary arrangements [illegible]. Also on return saw Sgt [illegible] & [illegible] who were being transferred [illegible] Bde R.F.A. for [illegible] [illegible]. Returned at 7.30 pm	[illegible]
		PM 10.0	On diary [illegible] &c. To see ADMS who told me to send [illegible] to 69th F.A. at [illegible] [illegible] [illegible] [illegible] [illegible] sanitary work & take charge of disinfectors [illegible] [illegible] [illegible] matter of [illegible] [illegible]. [illegible] [illegible] [illegible]	

1875 Wt. W593/826 1,000,000 4/15 J.B.C. & A. A.D.S.S./Forms/C. 2118.

Army Form C. 2118

Instructions regarding War Diaries and Intelligence Summaries are contained in F. S. Regs., Part II. and the Staff Manual respectively. Title Pages will be prepared in manuscript.

WAR DIARY
or
~~INTELLIGENCE SUMMARY~~
(Erase heading not required.)

Place	Date	Hour	Summary of Events and Information	Remarks and references to Appendices
	30.6.16	a.m. 9.0	Censoring letters. Inspected L/Cpl [illegible] & [illegible] approved to Allonville 69th F. Amb for constructing entrance to. L/Cpl [illegible] reported to office. At 10.30 set out on horse for Allonville. Staff Sergt overtook me on the road. We caught up S.S. party about half way. Arrived at D.R.S. about 11.40. Saw Capt Pye Smith who was examining some patients. A little later O.C. 69th F.A. arrived. Inspected the water supply. A [illegible] at [illegible], followed the [illegible] & found it was pumped by R.F.C. Later found lorry water tank supply also. Present latrines of [illegible] drums etc are unsatisfactory so deep trench [illegible] to be constructed. Thresh Disinfector (horse drawn type) was being worked by 17th Div San Sec. The M.C.O. in charge said they had enough blankets to last for 15 days. Reported this to Col Walker. Had lunch with F. Amb. & carried on inspecting [illegible] of work. Sent Staff Sgt back for [illegible], who arrived about 4.30. He made enquiries at the [illegible] [illegible] informed supply [illegible] from [illegible]. Left at [illegible] & inspected lorry water tank carts, sending message back to Capt Pye Smith [illegible]. Arrived at Vaux about 7.45 pm. On with orders etc. At 9.30 pm [illegible] ADMS but was not able to ~~[illegible]~~ see ADMS till about 10.30 pm. He spoke re travelling cookers, saying the cooks were [illegible]. He instructed me to examine them carefully in the future. He also called attention to the latrines at 'C' [illegible] saying that merely [illegible] the [illegible] at [illegible] was not sufficient.	[initials]
		p.m. 11.0		
			Month/ Owing to continual movement, the work [illegible] has been somewhat upset. The chief matters of change have been the [illegible] out of two of the personnel at the [illegible] & the return of the attached men to their units. A course of instruction on water supply & water carts was given after a report on the water personnel & carts had been submitted to ADMS. The weather has been changeable	

1875 Wt. W593/826 1,000,000 4/15 J.B.C. & A. A.D.S.S./Forms/C. 2118.

23rd Division

23 July

40 San Sec

Vol II

CONFIDENTIAL

WAR DIARY OF

SANITARY SECTION 40, R.A.M.C.T

23rd DIVISION.

(Volume II)

July 1916

Instructions regarding War Diaries and Intelligence Summaries are contained in F. S. Regs., Part II. and the Staff Manual respectively. Title Pages will be prepared in manuscript.

WAR DIARY
or
~~INTELLIGENCE SUMMARY~~
(Erase heading not required.)

Army Form C. 2118

Place	Date	Hour	Summary of Events and Information	Remarks and references to Appendices
VAUX	1-7-16	a.m. 8.50	Censoring letters. Writing up diary for yesterday. Instructions to St. Sgt. to proceed to Allonville with spray ~~tubes to commence~~ further inspection of carts re condition of clampers. Wrote covering letter to HQ [illegible] re inspecting cookers & condition of clampers on carts. Inspected Headqrs. watercart which was unsatisfactory i.e. not clean. Men did not appear to know their work. Inspected some latrines not being used with Sgt. Ellington. Went to see Camp Commandant re water duty men. He showed me that war establishments made no provision for sanitary only 2 RAMC water duty men. He came [illegible] water cart with me. To see water cart belonging to Signals R.E. It was cleaned very well but requires more spares. [illegible] cage &c. Spoke Sgt. Major who said matter was [illegible] for. Inspected dismantled latrine [illegible] Sgt. Major [illegible] fatigue for the work. At 2.10 pm set out on bicycle to D.R.S. at Allonville [illegible] Staff Sgt. on journey. Saw Capt. Pye Smith who told me ADMS had instructed him not to continue with present method. To let me [illegible] completed stand & to turn other trenches into [illegible] jobs. Inspected some of the latrines of the Flying Corps. On way back saw O.C. 70th F.A. Asked him if he knew re motor tank supply of water. He said they were already using it. Inspected tanks which were fairly satisfactory but [illegible] still required. Inspected [illegible] of 12 DLI with Lt [illegible] & [illegible] [illegible] for purpose intended. In one case [illegible] were in [illegible] compartment & in another compartment — a [illegible] compartment. Also inspected ones of the 11th N.F. but these appeared satisfactory. On return found that orders were about [illegible] saying that we must move at 7pm. Saw ADMS who instructed me to pack up. Later received instructions from him at [illegible] [illegible] was given final directions for move. Set out at 9.30pm with St. Sgt. 8 men with 3 bicycles. [illegible] proceeded at 9.15pm with [illegible] Sgt. Ellington [illegible]. Marched in one hour spells for [illegible] with ten minute rests after a 3/4 hr spell with 1 hr rest. Weather, fine.	[initials]
BAIZIEUX ~~[illegible]~~	2-7-16	a.m. 4.45	Arrived at Baizieux at 4.45 & after little difficulty found Sgt. Ellington [illegible] at [illegible]. No billets or covered accommodation available so at 5.30 we bivouacked in field near of Chateau. At 7.30 am with Sgt. Ellington [illegible] what water supplies available. Only one well found [illegible] a total supply was given at opposite [illegible]. Saw ADMS at 10.30 who told me to try & find billets which I promised to do but up to 1pm was not successful so gave it up. Selected a field for [illegible] & personnel & [illegible] moved to it. [illegible] at 6pm. At 3.30 – 5.0 men at work on [illegible]. Capt. Gill came round at about 6.30 said probably not moving to-night. [illegible] As I was not feeling well saw Gill who said he would let me know if ADMS wanted to see me. Later with Gill to see if I could obtain a billet but found it had already been taken.	[initials]
		p.m. 10.30	Men bivouacked in field. Weather, fine	

1875 Wt. W593/826 1,000,000 4/15 J.B.C. & A. A.D.S.S./Forms/C. 2118.

Instructions regarding War Diaries and Intelligence Summaries are contained in F. S. Regs., Part II. and the Staff Manual respectively. Title Pages will be prepared in manuscript.

WAR DIARY
or
~~INTELLIGENCE SUMMARY~~

(Erase heading not required.)

Army Form C. 2118

Place	Date	Hour	Summary of Events and Information	Remarks and references to Appendices
~~[illegible]~~ DAIZIEUX	3.7.16	A.M. 9.0	To make enquiries re water supply here. To see Maire with Mr Corpl. No infectious cases to report. To 26th F.A. to make enquiries re water but could obtain no information. Proceeded to [illegible] near Mairie & there saw a [illegible] Batt. [illegible] who said he was informed by 26th F.A. [illegible] responsible for [illegible] [illegible] [illegible], that water was pumped from [illegible]. To [illegible] found pumping station, R.E. Capt. in charge. Sources are open wells, the water being pumped to tanks at [illegible] only. Pump capacity about 1000 galls per hour. Are daily pumping 10 hrs. On to [illegible] Wood to see M.O. [illegible] [illegible] re his suggestion as to a [illegible] [illegible] [illegible] out he was out. [illegible] [illegible] inspected but was [illegible]. The latrines of the 22nd Bde were of [illegible] types, covered pit with liquid, [illegible] [illegible] [illegible]. The [illegible] were surrounding were in a very filthy state and Staff Capt. [illegible] [illegible]. Water supply obtained from taps on village of [illegible]. 71st F. Amb. [illegible] just arrived. The water supply for ambulance was from [illegible] supply near encampment. The infantry units not allowed to draw from these. Returned about [illegible] [illegible] office work — afternoon [illegible] A.D.M.S. [illegible] of sanitation in [illegible]. Capt. [illegible] [illegible] in re man for D.D.M.S. [illegible] [illegible] and inspected [illegible] grounds with Sgt. [illegible]. Made complaint as to condition of [illegible] to Capt. [illegible] R.E. [illegible] the [illegible] [illegible] [illegible] [illegible] [illegible] [illegible] [illegible] to [illegible] [illegible] [illegible].	[initials]
		P.M. 10.0	In evening saw A.D.M.S. Capt. 69th F. Amb. there who said personnel had been left at [illegible]. [illegible] [illegible] for O.C. [illegible] of A.D.M.S. and Ambulance could fill [illegible]. A.D.M.S. very busy [illegible] [illegible]	
	4.7.16	A.M. 8.45	Owing to [illegible] [illegible] [illegible] at camp [illegible] [illegible] [illegible]. To inspect [illegible] of D.R.S. on way met A.D.M.S. who hailed me & instructed me to proceed to A.D.S. Albert & [illegible] [illegible] [illegible] [illegible] F.A. [illegible] return. Proceeded to Albert in ambulance with Sgt. [illegible] + [illegible] who were proceeding to [illegible] [illegible] [illegible] [illegible] hospital there under instruction from A.D.M.S. Before leaving [illegible] I instructed Staff Sergt. to load lorry & proceed with remainder of section to [illegible] [illegible]. After arriving at D.S. at Albert I proceeded to A.D.S. where I saw Capt. [illegible] who said C.O. was in [illegible] [illegible] would send messenger to find him. [illegible] [illegible] about this & then returned to Albert where I found O.C. [illegible] F.A. just [illegible] going off. A.D.M.S. arrived. Returned to [illegible] [illegible] with A.D.M.S. in his car. Saw Capt. [illegible] later & came on with him to Dernancourt for billets. Found same.	[initials]
DERNANCOURT		A.M. 12.30	In evening saw A.D.M.S. who instructed me to attach the remaining portion of section to A.D.S. at Becourt Chateau & at [illegible] [illegible] & Dernancourt Ambulances. [illegible] [illegible] Raned in ~~[illegible]~~.	
	5.7.16	A.M. 8.30	To 71st F. Amb. to make arrangements about sanitation as instructed by A.D.M.S. last night. A.D.M.S. called about 9 o'clock. With Col. [illegible] in [illegible] billets etc. To 70th F Amb. to inspect work ~~[illegible]~~. Also superintended fitting of seats in lorry for wounded. In afternoon proceeded to A.D.S. Becourt Chateau. With S. Sgt. inspected area, which was in a very insanitary state. The yard near D. Room was full of garbage &c.	[initials]

1875 Wt. W593/826 1,000,000 4/15 J.B.C. & A. A.D.S.S./Forms/C. 2118.

Instructions regarding War Diaries and Intelligence Summaries are contained in F. S. Regs., Part II. and the Staff Manual respectively. Title Pages will be prepared in manuscript.

WAR DIARY

or

~~INTELLIGENCE~~ SUMMARY

(Erase heading not required.)

Army Form C. 2118

Place	Date	Hour	Summary of Events and Information	Remarks and references to Appendices
	Continued 5.4.16		Returned to 70 F. Amb. Assisted unloading ambulances. O.C. 70th F Amb. requested me to obtain German prisoners which had inadvertently been placed there. In connection with same [illegible] ADMS 3rd Corps. Took 10 German prisoners (slightly wounded) to Belle Vue farm in horse ambulance, handing them over to A.P.M. On return journey picked up an R.F.A. man who had broken his leg & took him to the Div. Amb. at Meault. Arrived back about 2.30 am	[initials]
		A.M. 4.0	Assisted in unloading ambulances &c, having [illegible] for men from [illegible] including Valient	
	6.4.16	AM 8.30	On instructions proceeded in lorry to 12th DIV. ADMS at [illegible] to obtain stretchers, blankets & but on reporting to him found he had none to spare. I then went on to DDMS at Montigny [illegible] he instructed me to return to 12th Div. as further arrangements had been made about them. Returned to ADMS 12th Div. who instructed the ADMS 12th Div handing over equipment &c me to proceed to Albert for the [illegible]. Returned about 8.30 pm	[initials]
		A.M. 2.30	Reported to ADMS office at 10 pm but he did not come back till after 2 am. Walter Brown	
	7.4.16	A.M. 9.30	Proceeded to ADMS office. Received instructions from him to proceed ADMS 12th DIV. for more equipment. On arrival he told me to go to [illegible] Wood & draw it. Returned about 1 pm & found ADMS had just [illegible]. Saw him about 2.30 pm he instructed me to proceed with some & lorry to 69th F. Amb. at Fricourt. Reported for duty to O.C. 69th F Amb. at Fricourt [illegible] up [illegible]. He asked me to act as Quarter master to [illegible] After a while a number of slightly wounded cases [illegible] but managed to get them away on lorries. On approval of O.C. 69th F Amb. returned to Dernancourt for the night at 11 pm. Walter [illegible]	[initials]
	8.4.16	am. 6.0	To 71st F Amb to catch an ambulance returning to Fricourt. Also to R.E. dump for ladders for lorries. Waited till 7.15 am but no car came so proceeded on cycle to Fricourt. Returned in an ambulance later for rations to 71st F Amb. Generally assisting &c. Did not return to billet but stayed at ambulance all night. Walter [illegible]	[initials]

1875 Wt. W593/826 1,000,000 4/15 J.B.C. & A. A.D.S.S./Forms/C. 2118.

Instructions regarding War Diaries and Intelligence Summaries are contained in F. S. Regs., Part II. and the Staff Manual respectively. Title Pages will be prepared in manuscript.

WAR DIARY
or
INTELLIGENCE SUMMARY

(Erase heading not required.)

Army Form C. 2118

Place	Date	Hour	Summary of Events and Information	Remarks and references to Appendices
FRICOURT	9.7.16		At 69th F. Amb searching for material, [illegible]. To Dernancourt to arrange for rations etc. Stayed at Ambulance assisting in small things. Inspected water supply. [signature]	[initials]
	10.7.16		At 69th F. Amb Watched fight for Contalmaison from top of hill. Spoke RE Corporal in charge of water [illegible] & suggested they should be cleaned out. He said he would speak to his officer. Returned to Dernancourt at 10.10 pm with lorry & 10 wounded in view of move tomorrow. [signature]	[initials]
	11.7.16		Received note from 69th F. Amb at 7.30 am for lorry. Sent it off at once, followed a little later in an ambulance. On arrival at Fricourt found that note was sent to O.C. 69th F. Amb as he was [illegible]. Waited till 11.15 am then returned in lorry as it was not required & the section had to move.	[initials]
ST. GRATIEN			Moved to St GRATIEN. Reported to ADMS at 9.30 pm who instructed me to carry out sanitary work at D.R.S. BAIZIEUX. 69th F. Amb. [signature]	
	12.7.16	9 AM	Per Ford Amb. (ADMS) proceeded to BAIZIEUX to 69th F. Amb D.R.S. with Sgt. [illegible] & 2 men. Inspected camp and noted [illegible] what to get on with. Three other men joined Sgt. [illegible] car sent for them. In afternoon commenced to get up clerical work which had been practically neglected since move from BAIZIEUX on the 2nd. In evening cycled to DRS again & saw Lt. Berry 11 W Yks on my way. Inspected works at DRS & returned in ambulance with Capt Silt.	[initials]
		10.30 AM	Saw ADMS at 10 pm & wrote out list of structures required at DRS & should be erected by RE. [signature]	

1875 Wt. W593/826 1,000,000 4/15 J.B.C. & A. A.D.S.S./Forms/C. 2118.

Instructions regarding War Diaries and Intelligence Summaries are contained in F. S. Regs., Part II. and the Staff Manual respectively. Title Pages will be prepared in manuscript.

WAR DIARY

or

~~INTELLIGENCE SUMMARY~~

(Erase heading not required.)

Army Form C. 2118

Place	Date	Hour	Summary of Events and Information	Remarks and references to Appendices
	13.4.16	A.M. 9.0	Capt. Bell came to office with telegram from D.D.M.S. saying St GRATIEN must be [illegible] – sanitary [illegible] by Sanitary Section. [illegible] a little while for ADMS but as he did not come I proceeded in ambulance to bring men back from D.R.S. at BAIZIEUX. Capt [illegible] Nicholson to [illegible] 64th F Amb & told Capt [illegible] what I proposed doing in regard to sanitary work there. Returned with Sgt. [illegible] and Capt Penfold. Capt [illegible] reported sick. In morning with Bell to see Town Major re the D.D.M.S. telegram. At 2 pm reported to Town Major's office [illegible] visited the various billets, latrines &c. – the village [illegible] [illegible] by [illegible] in regard to [illegible] work. Evening [illegible] &c. Saw Town Major & [illegible] & made complaint re condition of area around the cook houses [illegible]. Pte Buxton wanted to make application for transfer to Intelligence Service. Inspecting work in progress on latrines &c. Capt Bell to [illegible] re labour for work of [illegible]. Saw ADMS who instructed me to [illegible] who detailed [illegible] for this work. Saw [illegible] sanitation in village. Saw Col Wilkinson [illegible] slight [illegible]	[illegible]
		P.M. 10.45	Camp Commandant.	
	14.4.16	A.M. 9.0	Inspecting work in progress. [illegible] Interpreter to see [illegible] (but he was away) re employment of civilian labour in accordance with instructions received last night from Col Wilkinson. Spoke Town Major re [illegible] re cook houses not being removed & also no men on fatigue work. ADMS said he had instructed me to draw up a written report on the sanitation scheme. Visited latrines &c in conjunction with same. Drew up & sent in report by 3.30 pm. Capt Bell came & requested definite materials required & also labour. [illegible] sent [illegible] to him. In evening proceeded to DRS 64th F Amb at BAIZIEUX. Work more or less completed except ablution benches. Instructed Pte Nicholson to return tomorrow. Saw ADMS as he was going to dinner & he asked that lorry be placed at disposal of 64th F Amb tomorrow. He said there was no occasion to report to him this evening. [illegible]	[illegible]
		A.M. 10.15	Left office	

1875 Wt. W593/826 1,000,000 4/15 J.B.C. & A. A.D.S.S./Forms/C. 2118.

Army Form C. 2118

Instructions regarding War Diaries and Intelligence Summaries are contained in F. S. Regs., Part II. and the Staff Manual respectively. Title Pages will be prepared in manuscript.

WAR DIARY
or
~~INTELLIGENCE SUMMARY~~

(Erase heading not required.)

Place	Date	Hour	Summary of Events and Information	Remarks and references to Appendices
	15.7.16	A.M. 9.0	Inspected work of construction in village. Asked ADMS and [illegible] for me for further details for sanitation report of village, especially re wells. Saw RE Signals & complained to [illegible]. Also re men [illegible] especially in hedges. Sgt [illegible] accompanied me round. In afternoon & evening also inspected work. To Molliens-au-Bois inspected billets [illegible] Yorks. Saw M.O. but he had a bad ankle so was accompanied by sanitary corporal. Saw L/Cpl [illegible] & arranged to inspect 69th Bde units with him to-morrow. Sgt Chapman & Pte [illegible] reported to Section from 23rd Bde. Capt Bell came in in evening & said 15 men from D.R.S. to be attached for fatigues. These would be reporting to-morrow. [illegible]	[initials]
		P.M. 10.15	Saw ADMS & he spoke re water carts & "P.H." I reported re Signals R.E. Insisted that men might finish work at noon to-morrow to which he agreed. [signature]	
	16.7.16	A.M. 9.0	To Field Ambulance at Headqrs. To MOLLIENS-AU-BOIS to inspect 69th Bde particularly in regard to water carts & latrines. Met L/Cpl [illegible] there at 10.15 who accompanied me. Saw M.O. of 11th W. Yorks & 9th Yorks. Drew up report on same for ADMS. Visited Brigade again in afternoon. Saw Capt Bell there. In evening [illegible] men & drawing up report above etc. 1 Sgt & 18 O.R. reported for duty from D.R.S. in the afternoon. Read out G.R.O. 1683 [illegible] in grounds, also told men that ADMS had congratulated me on the way the Section had recently worked.	[initials]
		P.M. 10.0	Saw ADMS & handed him report of 69th Bde. He gave me permission to visit AMIENS. [signature]	
	17.7.16	A.M. 9.0	Saw O.C. 9th S. Staffs & made complaint re his men fouling hedges. [illegible] to Amiens. In afternoon inspecting sanitation work in village, also accompanied part of time by [illegible] [illegible] of this work etc. Four more men reported from D.R.S.	[initials]
		P.M. 10.30	In evening saw D.D.M.S. who instructed me to use lorry for drawing timber for 69th F. Amb. Told Adjutant R.E. (but he had gone) re authority for same. [signature]	

1875 Wt. W593/826 1,000,000 4/15 J.B.C. & A. A.D.S.S./Forms/C. 2118.

Instructions regarding War Diaries and Intelligence Summaries are contained in F. S. Regs., Part II. and the Staff Manual respectively. Title Pages will be prepared in manuscript.

WAR DIARY
or
~~INTELLIGENCE SUMMARY~~
(Erase heading not required.)

Army Form C. 2118

Place	Date	Hour	Summary of Events and Information	Remarks and references to Appendices
	18.4.16	A.M. 9.0	With Sgt. Chapman to Warloy [illegible] inspected 8Y [illegible] with M.O. Report [illegible] sent in to ADMS also visited & inspected 8K.O.Y.L.I. in afternoon with their M.O. Inspected village with view to a scheme of sanitation. Returned at 6.45 pm. [illegible] Amb [illegible] Inspected village [illegible] in morning before proceeding to [illegible].	
		P.M. 11.0	Saw ADMS & he asked for reports on villages separately. [illegible]	[illegible]
	19.4.16	A.M. 9.0	A.D.M.S. came in re supply of bricks. Instructed Sgt. Chapman to go to [illegible] to carry on drawing up sanitation scheme for that place. Proceeded to Amiens after a little trouble found bricks could be obtained from [illegible] 12 Boulevard [illegible], his works were at [illegible] - [illegible] Amiens & [illegible] 30 francs per 1000. Returned via [illegible]. Arrived back 1 [illegible]. In afternoon ADMS came in [illegible] [illegible] re [illegible] at rear of his [illegible]. Instructed Sgt. [illegible] to clear up. Owing to [illegible] Amb. not [illegible] [illegible] [illegible] driver was ill. Cycled to [illegible] [illegible] met Sgt. Chapman who returned with me. Saw T[own] Major re [illegible] [illegible] [illegible] [illegible] [illegible] dump. [illegible] [illegible] [illegible] about 6 pm. [illegible] [illegible] report [illegible] for the scheme. [illegible] [illegible] came in [illegible]	
		P.M. 11.20	[illegible] [illegible] [illegible] [illegible]. Saw ADMS in his [illegible] at 11 pm [illegible] he was [illegible] [illegible] me to [illegible] report on [illegible]. [illegible] [illegible] [illegible]	
	20.4.16	A.M. 9.0	[illegible] [illegible] to PIERREGOT to investigate re epidemic of chicken pox. Saw O.C. 40th F. Amb who reported one case definite, one suspected, one reported recovered. [illegible] [illegible] [illegible] daughter [illegible] the schoolmistress [illegible] neither had known of any cases [illegible] in the village. Saw T. Major [illegible] had not heard of any cases. He gave me a map for use in drawing up Sanit. scheme. In afternoon inspected some of the works here. Proceeded to PIERREGOT again to continue inspecting village for report. It is not an easy matter [illegible] out [illegible] [illegible] [illegible]. Returned at 6 pm. Reported to ADMS after seeing [illegible] RE re bricks. Was told instructions to be issued for more tomorrow.	
		P.M. 10.15	[illegible] ADMS re [illegible] of chicken pox epidemic at PIERREGOT [illegible] [illegible] [illegible] [illegible] daughter [illegible] [illegible] schoolmistress without them having heard or known of any case. [illegible]	[illegible]

1875 Wt. W593/826 1,000,000 4/15 J.B.C. & A. A.D.S.S./Forms/C. 2118.

Instructions regarding War Diaries and Intelligence Summaries are contained in F. S. Regs., Part II. and the Staff Manual respectively. Title Pages will be prepared in manuscript.

Army Form C. 2118

WAR DIARY
or
INTELLIGENCE SUMMARY
(Erase heading not required.)

Place	Date	Hour	Summary of Events and Information	Remarks and references to Appendices
ST GRATIEN	21-7-16	A.M. 9.0	Clearing up office work & sorting out material to hand over to T. Major which had been left over from the work carried out by Section. The Section while at this village had constructed 3 new latrines & reconstructed 3 as well as putting in 3 public urinals & urinals at each of the latrines. [illegible] area had been cleaned & [illegible] [illegible] indicating directions to water tank, latrines, urinals &c. Two incinerators were also built of petrol tins. Preparations for move. The lorry furnished with first load at 10 a.m. which included some ADMS material. Sgt [illegible] + 2 privates [illegible] & 2 men of [illegible] proceeded on lorry with Interpreter Corpl. The remainder of section with attached men moved off at 2.30 pm not waiting for lorry. Sgt Chapman & 3 privates left behind to come along with lorry's 2nd load. The march was carried out in easy stages (15 minutes spells & 5 minutes rests) & we arrived at Henencourt at about 6 pm. No men fell out. Adj [illegible] spoke re report of [illegible] billet. Reported to ADMS office at 10 pm but he was not expected. Received instructions from ADMS to send Corpl Oliver [illegible] to office in morning. [illegible]	[illegible]
HENENCOURT	22-7-16	A.M. 9.0	Diary &c. Inspected village. Latrines are plentiful & well constructed but there are large accumulations of rubbish which requires clearing. Inspected water supply at Chateau. Saw Capt Bell who mentioned re drawing stretchers for D.R.S. [illegible] ADMS instructed me to draw 2000. Saw Adj R.E. re drawing 1000 which C.R.E. approved. [illegible] Staff Sgt at midday re arrangement of men, as men did not appear to be properly placed. Tried to find where cart was which had been previously used for refuse collection. Saw ADMS at 6 pm. He instructed me re [illegible] as above, re sending [illegible] to D.R.S. & also that I could take over baths at Chateau. Office work. [illegible]	[illegible]
	23-7-16	A.M. 9.0	Censoring letters &c. To baths & found men cleaning up. With Sgt. Chapman inspected water carts of 101 & 102 RE & 69 Bde M.G.C. The 102 & 69 Bde were short of B.P. but otherwise the carts were in very fair condition. Corpl Gunner reported to me but had nothing of note. [illegible] his attention to condition of camp 69 M.G.C. & 101 RE. Saw Sergt 69th F. Amb. R.A.M.C. [illegible] for refuse cart. In morning also with Interpreter re refuse cart. [illegible] found one at [illegible] in field S. of village. In afternoon at Baths. 140 O.R. & [illegible] had baths from 3.30 – 6.30. Tubs [illegible] all water had to be hand carried which made things slow. Diary, correspondence &c.	[illegible]
		P.M. 10.30	Saw ADMS who instructed me to send 2 personnel + 5 attached men to [illegible] tomorrow. [illegible]	

1875 Wt. W593/826 1,000,000 4/15 J.B.C. & A. A.D.S.S./Forms/C. 2118.

Army Form C. 2118

Instructions regarding War Diaries and Intelligence Summaries are contained in F. S. Regs., Part II. and the Staff Manual respectively. Title Pages will be prepared in manuscript.

WAR DIARY
or
~~INTELLIGENCE SUMMARY~~
(Erase heading not required.)

Place	Date	Hour	Summary of Events and Information	Remarks and references to Appendices
	24-7-16	A.M. 8.45	arranging for party [illegible] Bécourt Château. [illegible] Hopwood [illegible] at [illegible] to 70th Bde. To Bull's after seeing Adj. RE [illegible] account for bricks for C.R.E. [illegible] Saw [illegible] re [illegible] boilers at [illegible] had been repaired [illegible] improvement on yesterday's [illegible] this morning from 69th F. Amb [illegible] not satisfactory [illegible] was not successful. On horseback to [illegible] incinerators [illegible] village [illegible] T. Major [illegible] away so I could not see him. [illegible] Sergt. [illegible] reported water supply [illegible] Camp Comm. who said I could have use of G.S. wagon for water [illegible] 193rd A.S.C. also 192 & 191 Co. A.S.C. at [illegible]. [illegible] all had been [illegible]. Otherwise sanitary arrangements [illegible] as well as conditions permitted. Censoring letters &c.	[initials]
		P.M. 10.0	Saw M.O. RE re [illegible] 138th Co he said he had not arranged for same. Saw ADMS who said that I should be [illegible] at [illegible] when we were again in the line. [signature]	
	25/7/16	A.M. 9.0	Censored letters. To see Adj. RE re quicklime supply. To Bull's [illegible] re sending men to Bull's. To [illegible] [illegible] re water cart particulars. In afternoon inspecting bathing work. Clearing up office work. To CRE office [illegible] who said [illegible] there was no supply of quicklime. To ADMS office [illegible] movement orders. ADMS said I should arrange [illegible] to see O.C. 69th F. Amb. [illegible] re lorry. To [illegible] with ADMS re [illegible] information. To see O.C. 69th F. Amb [illegible] arranged re lorry also [illegible] 1 NCO & 7 men [illegible] [signature]	[initials]
	26/7/16	A.M. 9.0	arrangements for parties to [illegible] advanced area. Correspondence, censoring letters &c. Lorry did not arrive back from 69th F. Amb. till [illegible] hence move was delayed considerably. Lorry [illegible] equipment [illegible] at Albert about 5 p.m. [illegible]	
ALBERT			[illegible] to T. Major's office [illegible] No 128 Rue de Bapaume for men at No 7 Rue [illegible] for office & [illegible]	[initials]
		P.M. 10.30	Reported to ADMS [illegible] Corps scheme particulars [illegible] At T. Major's office [illegible] T. Major asked me to be at his office at 10 [illegible] tomorrow [illegible] Sanitary Officer of Albert [signature]	

1875 Wt. W593/826 1,000,000 4/15 J.B.C. & A. A.D.S.S./Forms/C. 2118.

Instructions regarding War Diaries and Intelligence Summaries are contained in F. S. Regs., Part II. and the Staff Manual respectively. Title Pages will be prepared in manuscript.

WAR DIARY

or

~~INTELLIGENCE SUMMARY~~

(Erase heading not required.)

Army Form C. 2118.

Place	Date	Hour	Summary of Events and Information	Remarks and references to Appendices
	27.7.16	A.M. 9.0	Office work. 9.45 — To Town Major. Met there [illegible] Sanitary Officer [illegible] the A.D.M.S. re matter of work in Albert. Both morning & afternoon with Capt Etherington on sanitation scheme (Corps III). [illegible] at 7 p.m. & on with second plan for scheme. Office work &c. Town shelled.	[illegible]
		P.M. 11.0	To see A.D.M.S. who instructed me to carry on cleaning out [illegible] dug outs before carrying on with Corps scheme. [illegible]	
	28.7.16	A.M. 9.0	Office work. Town being shelled, as also during night. At artillery dug outs [illegible] around supervising cleaning up &c. An area about 100 yds away was in a deplorable condition in the matter of food refuse. On arrival back in afternoon enquired of a [illegible] in charge of G S wagon removing material left this morning. He said [illegible] were not coming now. Stopped men cleaning up. Spoke A.D.M.S. — warning re no notification being sent. In morning saw Camp Commandant who handed over a party of 50 infantry fatigue party. In evening matter arose re sudden removal of	[illegible]
		A.M. 12.30	men from [illegible] A.D.M.S. having arranged about it [illegible] leaving while for instruction as to withdrawing my men. [illegible] his instructions to do so. I thought I had carried out instructions. The day was wasted as regards Corps scheme in view of [illegible] work at artillery dugouts. [illegible]	[illegible]

2449 Wt. W14957/M90 750,000 1/16 J.B.C. & A. Forms/C.2118/12.

Instructions regarding War Diaries and Intelligence Summaries are contained in F. S. Regs., Part II. and the Staff Manual respectively. Title Pages will be prepared in manuscript.

WAR DIARY
or
~~INTELLIGENCE SUMMARY~~
(Erase heading not required.)

Army Form C. 2118.

Place	Date	Hour	Summary of Events and Information	Remarks and references to Appendices
	29.7.16	AM 9.0	Censoring letters. To site of encampment for Divisional Headqrs. choosing positions for latrines &c arranging arrangements for materials also getting work in hand. In afternoon with Sergt Ellingham inspecting area for Corps Sanitation Scheme, fixing final positions for latrines &c. In evening to D. H. encampment superintending works in progress. S Sergt returned from [illegible]	[illegible]
		PM 11.0	To see A.D.M.S. but nothing of importance to report or as regards instructions.	
			Weather fine hot.	
	30.7.15	A.M. 9.0	To Town Major's office to see re change of billets. Met also Sanitary Officer who [illegible] as to supplying tools for the personnel &c. Later to see A.D.M.S. who gave me chit to ask R.E. to supply tools required. He also instructed me to attach [illegible] L. D. men. In afternoon with Sergt Ellingham continuing inspection of Corps Scheme Area. Saw O.C. 41st F Amb at [illegible] [illegible] inspected latrines. Arranged with him for medical inspection of L D men. Returned at 4. 0 p.m. S. Sergt + Sergt Ellingham [illegible] L. D. men at [illegible]	[illegible]
		PM 10.30	Saw A.D.M.S. discussed re Camp stores for personnel. Nothing of importance.	
			Weather fine, very hot	
	31.7.15	A.M. 9.0	Censoring letters, office work &c. To D. H. camp. Saw Adj. R.E. who offered material for latrines &c. Inspected work & [illegible] to Capt [illegible] re same. Town Major this morning gave permission for me to take over other billets. Billets removed from Rue [illegible] + Rue de Bapaume to Rue de [illegible] No 3 + 5. In afternoon to see "[illegible]" party work [illegible] to complete Corps Sanitation Scheme inspection. Office work [illegible]. Pte Nicholson reported at office; water notice boards not received.	[illegible]
		PM 10.30	Saw A.D.M.S. but nothing of importance to report. He asked when scheme (Corps) would be completed.	
			Weather very hot	

2449 Wt. W14957/M90 750,000 1/16 J.B.C. & A. Forms/C.2118/12.

August 1916

23rd Div

WAR DIARY OF

SANITARY SECTION 40
R.A.M.C. (T)

FROM AUGUST 1ST TO AUGUST 31ST 1916

(VOLUME 12)

Army Form C. 2118.

Instructions regarding War Diaries and Intelligence Summaries are contained in F. S. Regs., Part II. and the Staff Manual respectively. Title Pages will be prepared in manuscript.

WAR DIARY
or
~~INTELLIGENCE SUMMARY~~

(Erase heading not required.)

Place	Date	Hour	Summary of Events and Information	Remarks and references to Appendices
ALBERT	1-8.16	A.M. 9.0	Capt. [illegible] came to office in regard to sanitary condition of [illegible] camp. Returned with him [illegible] saw ADMS who said camp was a permanent one & must be fitted up with good sanitary arrangements. He gave me chit for C.R.E. for materials. Saw C.R.E. & [illegible] from me to draw materials [illegible] which ADMS suggested [illegible] purchase. C.R.E. got me authority to collect from damaged houses. [illegible] [illegible] [illegible] [illegible] [illegible] station where woman [illegible] [illegible] Arranging for calling back [illegible] [illegible] from [illegible]. On arrival back [illegible] [illegible] arranging for collection of bricks, [illegible] [illegible] [illegible] to get men on work. Arranged with Camp Comdt's M.C.O. for G.S. waggon for bricks. Superintending work [illegible] M.O. [illegible] R.E. At 5.30 p.m. proceeded on cycle [illegible] [illegible] Staff Sgt. [illegible] work [illegible] Saw also an officer of A.C. near one of the latrines who said his Colonel was complaining [illegible] [illegible] [illegible] [illegible] able to point out that latrines had only been opened [illegible] that morning [illegible] [illegible] to [illegible] of their camp. He then showed me a spot where horses were [illegible] [illegible] [illegible] mess. To 183 Bde R.F.A. waggon lines re [illegible] on [illegible] of sanitary report from M.O. [illegible] Cpl [illegible] [illegible] of artillery waggon lines in respect to [illegible]. Made arrangements for two [illegible] latrines to be constructed which would also form part of scheme. To 105 R.G.A. camp but Sgt [illegible] was away, saw L/Cpl [illegible]. Returned at 10.10 [illegible] Sgt [illegible] at office [illegible] [illegible] complaint.	[illegible]
		P.M. 10.45	To see ADMS. Spoke re report, he said he would see me tomorrow at [illegible] Slept in cellar [illegible] [illegible]. [illegible] [illegible] [illegible]	
	2.8.16	A.M. 9.0	On morning letters to [illegible] [illegible] Camp Commandant re [illegible] [illegible] [illegible] can be obtained. Drew 500 [illegible] from Field [illegible]. Inspected [illegible] camp with Sgt. [illegible] [illegible]. On with Corps [illegible] report [illegible] office work. In afternoon to see San Officer Albert re complaint by M.O. 13th D.L.I. re billets. Saw T. Major about matter as S.O. was out. Saw Cpls [illegible] & [illegible] re cleaning up billets &c, but 68th Bde were in the line & Cpl [illegible] said he would arrange with the S.O. to construct latrines for the 2 battalions now in Albert. Spoke to S.O. 14th Div.	[illegible]
		P.M. 8.0	Saw ADMS with Corps scheme at 7 pm [illegible] [illegible]	

Instructions regarding War Diaries and Intelligence Summaries are contained in F. S. Regs., Part II. and the Staff Manual respectively. Title Pages will be prepared in manuscript.

WAR DIARY
or
~~INTELLIGENCE SUMMARY~~

(Erase heading not required.)

Army Form C. 2118.

Place	Date	Hour	Summary of Events and Information	Remarks and references to Appendices
	3.8.16	A.M. 9.0	Amending Corps Sanitation Scheme Report as per A.D.M.S. suggestions. Answering letters &c. To see incinerator being built at Divl [illegible]. To [Brant?] area to inspect works with [illegible] Sergt. Chose a second site for manure dump. Returned about 2.15 pm. Entering diary &c. Inspecting Divl Camp with Sergt [Ettrington?]. Saw Capt Bill [illegible] re putting up drinking [boards?]. He showed me letter from Capt [Frowal?] RAMC 103rd Bde re complaint of latrines alteration. At 4.0 pm saw ADMS who instructed me to [illegible] M.O. 8th K.O.Y.L.I. re his telegram as to type of incinerators for his unit encamped near [Bécourt?], also to arrange for disinfection of 69th Bde clothing.	[initials]
		P.M. 10.0	To see 69th Bde re disinfection of men's clothing & made necessary arrangements. Instructed Capt [illegible] re same. Weather fine, not [illegible]	
	4.8.16	A.M. 8.45	Answering letters, office work &c. To [illegible] to meet Capt Bill. Found he had left [illegible] at [illegible] so followed him down. We proceeded to [illegible] Amb [illegible] & called at H.Q. "Field Amb. Hospital" [illegible] dugout they were occupying which was undoubtedly the finest I had seen. Proceeded on foot to see M.O. 8th K.O.Y.L.I. re his telegram as to type of incinerator he would use. Pointed out to him that in advanced position [illegible] it was more a military than a sanitary matter as doubtless an incinerator in that position would draw the enemy's fire. Inspected German trench latrine which was a very deep covered pit in a side trench & was evidently [illegible] by our troops. After leaving there we proceeded to Adv Post H.Q. [illegible] F Amb at [illegible] Wood & then on to A.D.S. 69th F Amb at Contalmaison. In both cases the dug outs were excellently made, the latter having some of the "rooms" lined with boarding. Inspected latrines & instructed [illegible] Nicholson to cut [illegible] at back end of trench of latrine in [illegible]. The latrine was one constructed by us of 3 openings with flaps. Returned [illegible] lunch with O.C. 69th F Amb at [Fricourt?]. In afternoon arrived back about 2.30 pm. Cleared up a few office matters. Dined mess. Proceeded to see Staff Sergt. Corps Scheme 3 Latrines completed as regards fly traps by ourselves, two completed by 103 Bde R.F.A. & another one commenced by us. Returned 5 pm. To see ADMS at 10 pm but not [illegible] report. Heavy bombardment proceeding, the sky being lit up with the flashes of the guns & bursting shells as well as by the various star shells of all colours (red, green, orange). Weather fine, water [illegible]	[initials]

2449 Wt. W14957/M90 750,000 1/16 J.B.C. & A. Forms/C.2118/12.

Instructions regarding War Diaries and Intelligence Summaries are contained in F. S. Regs., Part II. and the Staff Manual respectively. Title Pages will be prepared in manuscript.

WAR DIARY
or
INTELLIGENCE SUMMARY
(Erase heading not required.)

Army Form C. 2118.

Place	Date	Hour	Summary of Events and Information	Remarks and references to Appendices
	3/8/16	A.M. 9.0	Censored letters & inspected Foden Disinfector at work. Only two small quantities of shirts had been sent up to 9 o'clock. Send letter to Staff Captain to say that it would be impossible to get 4000 shirts done if sent at present rate viz. 138 & 189. Received wire from him saying he was telephoning units about the matter. Arrangements made with Staff Captain re 3 shifts of 8 hours each 2am – 10am – 10am – 4pm – 4pm – 10pm. 8 fatigue men to be sent per shift & I undertook to do 4000 shirts in the day. Inspected work in progress at Div[l] [illegible] camp. Rounded on cycle to find A.S.C. On way passed D.A.C. lines saw M.O. i/c mentioned re a second [illegible] [illegible] if he would send for one also re necessity for covering latrine pits. Got to 191 Co. A.S.C. saw O.C. this camp was evidently well supervised as kitchen had muslin for protection from flies, boxed covered latrines & properly constructed urinals [sketch: petrol tins, bully beef tins]. Men were not allowed to eat their meals near their bivouacs. He informed me that he had obtained some Stockholm tar from England (at his own expense) & found it invaluable for mixing with [illegible] for keeping flies away. care had to be taken to only smear the tar on. Tried to find [illegible] Co. A.S.C. but was not successful. The water cart of the 191 Co. was also in good condition. Spoke Staff Sgt. of San Sec of Australian Div. apparently your work was similar in most respects To Bécourt San. Area & spoke O.C. B. Batty 41st Bde RFA re constructing a latrine [illegible] incinerator. He promised to help in the matter but the O.C. remaining batteries of brigade said he would send my Staff Sgt. to see him re details of starting work. He complained as my experience also goes re difficulty of getting material for sanitary works. It is absurd that work is expected to be done yet material cannot be obtained for this work, thus increasing the difficulties in getting areas in a sanitary condition. Before going to 41st Bde saw Capt Woodhouse at 69th F. Amb. wagon lines & from there sent a note to Capt. [illegible] Smith to ask if he would medically [illegible] attached men. Inspected latrine [illegible] required a little attention as it was not fly proof. Saw O.C. Section [illegible] D.A.C. 15th Div. & asked him to only use official latrines. He also promised to build fly incinerators. I find units are very reluctant to [illegible] [illegible] sanitary construction. No undoubtedly if there are official latrines they should	[illegible]

2449 Wt. W14957/M90 750,000 1/16 J.B.C. & A. Forms/C.2118/12.

Instructions regarding War Diaries and Intelligence Summaries are contained in F. S. Regs., Part II. and the Staff Manual respectively. Title Pages will be prepared in manuscript.

Army Form C. 2118.

WAR DIARY
or
INTELLIGENCE SUMMARY

(Erase heading not required.)

Place	Date	Hour	Summary of Events and Information	Remarks and references to Appendices
	5/8/16 continued		Returned at 7.30 pm & found Rev. Chaplain waiting to see me re a Church parade tomorrow evening at 6 pm. I promised to try & arrange it. The Section has only attended one Church parade since coming to France, i.e. at Merris in September 1915. Pte Yarnold reported for duty from D.D.M.S. II Corps. He had been engaged there for months on clerical work. Pte Hopwood reported for duty from 2nd Army H.Q. yesterday. He had been engaged in intelligence work as he has knowledge of French & German. Evidently neither of these men are strong. Sent for Sergt Elkington to make arrangements for tomorrow. 1500 shirts only have been sent for disinfection. Exact total 1512.	[illegible]
		PM 10.0	To see A.D.M.S. he said D.D.M.S. approved sanitation scheme. Arranged with Capt Bell for medical inspection of L.D. men temporarily attached to Section. 31 to report tomorrow at 9 a.m. The [illegible] at [illegible] both [illegible] there. The shelling of ALBERT at night seemed much heavier than we have yet experienced. Weather fine	
	6/8/16 Sunday	9 AM 0	Spent the morning in general work viz inspected equipment, letters from [illegible] & other clerical work. Inspected incinerators at work. In afternoon called at camps of 192 & 193 Cos A.S.C. re manure spreaders & officers of these companies said they would be useful. O.C. M.V.C. also wanted one & I instructed them to send [illegible] for them. Proceeded on horse after visiting above camps to see Staff Sergt & party at Bécourt. During time [illegible] this morning work delayed. [illegible] sanitation to men bathing in wood. Returned in time to see Church parade party march off to church. [illegible] & Interpreter came in at 7 o'clock. Said Capt Bell told him we were to move at once. Capt [illegible] with written instructions to this effect. [illegible] and all troops are now ordered not to billet in ALBERT owing to the shelling. A splinter from a shell had gone thro' bivouac sheet of Sgt Elkington last night but fortunately did not touch him. To see O.C. of [illegible] near bivouac ground, & found map reference in instructions practically agreed to a [illegible] position. The O.C. had no objection to our bivouacking at [illegible]. Taken [illegible] on [illegible] up [illegible].	[illegible]
		AM 10.0	Saw A.D.M.S. at 9.45 pm but nothing special to report. Received written instructions to meet O.C. San Sec 15th Div. Weather fine, very cool evening.	

2449 Wt. W14957/M90 750,000 1/16 J.B.C. & A. Forms/C.2118/12.

Instructions regarding War Diaries and Intelligence Summaries are contained in F. S. Regs., Part II. and the Staff Manual respectively. Title Pages will be prepared in manuscript.

WAR DIARY
or
INTELLIGENCE SUMMARY
(Erase heading not required.)

Army Form C. 2118.

Place	Date	Hour	Summary of Events and Information	Remarks and references to Appendices
	4.8.18	9.0 a.m.	Written instructions for L/Cpl Smith re his visit to Scots Redoubt. Fixing up business. Received message from Capt Bell to call at office, left camp & on arrival found D.C. San Sec 15th Div. there & was pleased to see it was Dawkins. He inspected records and afterwards proceeded to Corps Sanitation Scheme near Bécourt. He inspected workshop & also the two latrines in sub area 2. Ford car tyres gave out so we walked as far as wood near eastern boundary of area. He said scheme was a large thing & we agreed that Corps work such as this should be done [illegible] by a Corps unit as the work entailed meant less supervision of one's division. Since being in ALBERT I have had a considerable amount of work undertaken, viz Div[l] Incinerator, sanitary arrangements, Corps scheme, assistance to Town Major, 3 removals of billets. One of the chief difficulties has been to get material for Corps Scheme, if substantial progress is wanted certainly the material should be forthcoming. Section was also two men short & one with DDMS III Corps, & 1 with Corps Intelligence Dept. They returned yesterday for duty. At this moment personnel is as follows/ Incinerator Sergt. Cpl, 2 LCpls 2 Ptes (Bécourt) Bécourt 1 S Sergt 2 LCpls, 1 Pte, Town Major 1 LCpl 3 privates, Contalmaison 1 LCpl/ & together with 8 personnel attached to 3 Inf Bdes & Artillery makes up Section. Attached men as follows Incinerator 19 Bécourt 14 Contalmaison 4 & one as orderly for ADMS & Town Major = 38/ Number of latrines constructed at Corps Scheme are 12 seats, one 10 seats, one 8 seat, together with 2 - 8 seats which assisted by 103 Bde R.F.A. According to medical examination report 10 of L D attached to Section returned to their units to-day, being fit for duty. Two horses of the 12 were reported fit disposed of as follows, one to Reinforcement Camp as he was [illegible] the 9 R W F 19th Div. & a LCpl M.G.C. kept on. I was informed his unit was at BAIZIEUX where we move to tomorrow. Returned from inspecting Corps Scheme Area about 6pm. Arrangements for disposal of men fit for duty, arrangements for move, [illegible] billets, diary etc. till 6.30 pm. To see A.D.M.S at 4 o'clock, nothing of importance to report. LCpl Nicholson & 4 L.D. men returned from CONTALMAISON. These men resumed duty tomorrow S Sgt & party from BECOURT returned. Had occasion to mention to Staff Sgt. re his not carrying out work according to the scheme. Instructions issued for tomorrow/ Twelve more L.D. men reported for duty to replace those sent back Weather fine	

2449 Wt. W14957/M90 750,000 1/16 J.B.C. & A. Forms/C.2118/12.

Army Form C. 2118.

Instructions regarding War Diaries and Intelligence Summaries are contained in F. S. Regs., Part II. and the Staff Manual respectively. Title Pages will be prepared in manuscript.

WAR DIARY
or
INTELLIGENCE SUMMARY

(Erase heading not required.)

Place	Date	Hour	Summary of Events and Information	Remarks and references to Appendices
(ALBERT) to BAIZIEUX	8-8-16	A.M. 9.0	Lorry went to draw rations at usual time but returned to say rations could not be drawn before eleven. This meant delay for move. Lorry loaded [illegible] for rations proceeded to BAIZIEUX. It returned at 3pm in order to remove material (ADMS) at 3.15pm. Returned for third load at 5pm. Men at headquarters worked during day as usual remainder cleaning up old encampment, loading lorry &c. Owing to [illegible] numbers of [illegible] with them every Party (Section of L.D. men) moved off at 5pm. Men not fit for walking being conveyed on lorry. Arrived at BAIZIEUX at 7pm. Men fixed up in billets & [illegible] formed by [illegible]. Self & officer to old encampment. Instructions to Staff Sgt & Sgt Elkington for work tomorrow.	[initials]
		P.M. 10.0	Reported to A.D.M.S. at 10pm but nothing of importance to report. As mentioned many [illegible] works [illegible] or less stopped. Inspected Headqrs camp prior to leaving [illegible] 3 men & [illegible] had [illegible] left behind. Also on inspecting incinerator large amount of [illegible] required dispersing. Ordered same to be put in [illegible], as there was much combustible material in it. Weather – fine	
BAIZIEUX	9-8-16	A.M. 9.0	Office work. Answering letters, diary, going through papers &c. To 70th Bde Headqrs at Franvillers & handed 8 manure sprayers to Sgt Chapman for distribution to battalions. Also earlier saw O.C. 70th F. Amb [illegible] re sprayers & he asked for [illegible]. A[In afternoon Capt Bell came round re water tanks for Headqrs as water carts had gone on to [illegible] orders. After a little while saw [illegible] 3rd D.S.C. & he said he would loan his tank till tomorrow morning. Inspected Headqrs. Reported at A.D.M.S. office at 7pm but ADMS did not arrive. Saw Bell also C. Commandant & discussed re tank borrowed from 3rd D.S.C. & arrangements for men drawing same. O.C. told me many billets at AILLY-LE-HAUT-CLOCHER. Nothing else of importance. Weather – Rained last night & this morning. Dull, [illegible]]A	[initials]
	10-8-16	A.M. 9.0	Owing to rain moved from bivouac to old building. Clerical work. Calls as above A[ ]A B{ }B Inspected Headqrs area. Saw an officer [illegible] RE signals & made complaint re condition of latrines. He said they would receive immediate attention. Inspected Signals [illegible] & found same was in a satisfactory condition. Reported to ADMS office at 7pm but neither he nor Capt Bell was there. Reported at 10pm when C. Commandant came in but nothing of importance discussed. [illegible] officer joined me. Weather, fine B} }B	[initials]

2449 Wt. W14957/M90 750,000 1/16 J.B.C. & A. Forms/C.2118/12.

Instructions regarding War Diaries and Intelligence Summaries are contained in F. S. Regs., Part II. and the Staff Manual respectively. Title Pages will be prepared in manuscript.

WAR DIARY
or
~~INTELLIGENCE SUMMARY~~

(Erase heading not required.)

Army Form C. 2118.

Place	Date	Hour	Summary of Events and Information	Remarks and references to Appendices
BAIZIEUX TO AILLY-LE-HAUT-CLOCHER	11/8/16	A.M. 6.45 MIDNIGHT 12.0	To men's billet to inspect getting away. Men marched off under Salvage Co. [illegible] to HENENCOURT station under O.C. Salvage. Saw lorries picking up final materials & left with Croal [illegible] at Sgt Elkington + 2 men + 2 Gas men, for station at 8.15. Arrived at 9.45 am [illegible] which found party. Had lunch with Major [illegible] Adj R.E. [illegible] village. Train supposed to leave at 10 am — did not leave till 3.30 pm arrived LONGPRÉ 8.30 pm. The journey was very slow [illegible]. Obtained supper at Croal, [illegible] & self [illegible] to AILLY arriving about 10.15 pm. Saw Capt Bill near to billet. Lorry had arrived safely. O.C. Salvage & party arrived about 11.30 pm. Sgt & Cpl Smith had fallen out [illegible] (attended). All had reported the next morning except a L/Cpl. Sent a Corporal to see if he could find him. Some men found [illegible] up in billet after got to bed. The journey owing to the [illegible] very annoying. [illegible signature]	[illegible initials]
AILLY-LE-HAUT-CLOCHER	12/8/16	A.M. 9.30	Capt Bill came in re [illegible] of lorry remaining behind. Saw M.O. [illegible] who came [illegible] of my men who were sick. Sent out working parties &c. [illegible] Inspected equipment to be taken on lorry. With Sergt Elkington visited horse lines of following [illegible], 69th Bde [illegible], Signals, M.M.P. They were just moving off. Left instructions for [illegible] latrines filled in. Owing to short stays very little sanitary arrangements to be found. Saw ADMS about 10 pm [illegible] lorry also re [illegible]. [illegible signature]	[illegible initials]
AILLY-LE-HAUT-CLOCHER TO BAILLEUL TO FLETRE	13/8/16 14/8/16	A.M. 7.30	To see lorry loaded for journey left at 7.15. Returned to [illegible] to [illegible] 11 a.m. Reparations for moving off. Inspected billets. Moved off at 3 pm & arrived LONGPRÉ station 5.30 pm. [illegible] (45 mins – [illegible]) a complete journey in 75 minutes. [illegible] Train left about 6.30 pm. Woman charged 9 francs for 3 [illegible] which [illegible] declared [illegible]. Owing to train moving off unable to hand back some of the woman['s] cups &c. [illegible signature] Arrived station at 4.30 a.m. Marched off at 5.15 & reached Fletre 7.0 a.m. Found Sergt Elkington & party — [illegible] just outside village. Billet taken for me & [illegible] by AA & QMG. Found another billet also one for Gas Officer & a room for the mess. Laid down from 8.30 am to 10.30. To men's encampment [illegible] to [illegible] re water, sanitary arrangements [illegible] Elkington [illegible] to [illegible]	[illegible initials] [illegible initials]

Instructions regarding War Diaries and Intelligence Summaries are contained in F. S. Regs., Part II. and the Staff Manual respectively. Title Pages will be prepared in manuscript.

WAR DIARY
or
INTELLIGENCE SUMMARY
(Erase heading not required.)

Army Form C. 2118.

Place	Date	Hour	Summary of Events and Information	Remarks and references to Appendices
	14/8/16 continued		The well had pump & gearing left but motor had been removed. It would take some little time to get it up in working order, [illegible] probably short [illegible] to get matters under way. Met [illegible] & again looked at well. Saw C. Commandant about his men digging larger latrine trench. At office entering diary, letters &c. Inspecting village with [illegible]. Made mental note of large collection of petrol tins (empty). Saw A.D.M.S. & arranged to meet O.C. San. Sec. 41st Div. to-morrow [illegible] office. I to go over with him to Steenwerck in his car. Nothing else of moment. Weather: Slight showers.	[illegible]
FLETRE.	15/8/16	A.M. 8.45	At ADMS office at 9.0 a.m. & proceeded to Steenwerck with [illegible] O.C. 84th San. Sec. 41st Division, Lt. Vickers. He obtained loan of car & we proceeded to inspect some of the camps [illegible]. [illegible] LA ROMARIN [illegible] description of work. [illegible] similar to our previous experience in adjoining area. They [illegible] also undertake practically no constructional work. Water supply now chiefly drawn from an official supply pumped from the [illegible]. He handed me various papers re water & also a list of [illegible] of his men & agreements (copies) with Communes of [illegible] & Steenwerck. [illegible] I returned about 2 p.m. At office [illegible] with him [illegible] to his personnel's billets [illegible] for work in new area. Answering letters & getting out particulars &c. I spoke ADMS on following points/ Billeting	[illegible]
		P.M. 11.0	Saw A.D.M.S. & went to Gas Office [illegible]. [illegible] billeted at Steenwerck personnel from brigades [illegible]. Billets, he said [illegible] should have use of a car daily from F. Amb in Steenwerck. Civilians [illegible] employment of civilians on sanitation work. Agreements with Communes [illegible]. Weather, Showery	[illegible]
	16/8/16	A.M. 9.0	Further arrangements made for work in new area. Answering letters &c. Saw C Commandant as he was [illegible] billets [illegible]. Sent Cpl [illegible] in advance party to [illegible] to new area. Provided also [illegible] lorry to look for billets at STEENWERCK with [illegible]. Returned to FLETRE at [illegible] with the ADMS. Arrangements made for medical inspection of attached men to-morrow.	
		P.M. 10.15	After dinner fixing up arrangements to get work in new area &c. — Weather, Slight showers	

2449 Wt. W14957/M90 750,000 1/16 J.B.C. & A. Forms/C.2118/12.

Army Form C. 2118.

Instructions regarding War Diaries and Intelligence Summaries are contained in F. S. Regs., Part II. and the Staff Manual respectively. Title Pages will be prepared in manuscript.

WAR DIARY
or
INTELLIGENCE SUMMARY

(Erase heading not required.)

Place	Date	Hour	Summary of Events and Information	Remarks and references to Appendices
FLETRE TO STEENWERCK	17/8/16	A.M. 9.0	With Capt Gill at inspection of attached men. 22 certified fit for duty. Details for move. Proceeded on horse to new area & at BAILLEUL called at F. Cashier & drew 750 francs for Imprest A/c. Inspected water tank near [illegible] on the way & reached STEENWERCK at 12.30 pm. To men's billet & issued instructions. After lunch very heavy showers but left on foot to proceed to men's [illegible] billet. Saw O.C. 41 San Sec. & discussed re area. Returned on lorry with Sergt Elkington, the latter coming to Steenwerck owing to Sergt Chapman reporting sick. Arrived back 6.30 pm & making arrangements &c. & discussing with Sergt Elkington & Corpl Gunner re water supply. Drainage, [illegible] &c. To see ADMS. & asked re horses for refuse carts, arrangement of brigades – trenches, positions of A.D.S. &c. mentioned re water supply. Weather, Showery	E.J.H.
STEENWERCK	18.8.16	A.M. 9.0	To 41st F. Amb re men to return to their units. With M.O. to C.R.E. to inspect water supply at rear of mess. Refuse cart started work. Arrangements for sending of attached men back to their units independent of F. Amb. With Corpl Gunner in Ford to A.D.S. [illegible] & on tour of inspection of water in the wood & trenches. Found system of a [illegible] supply with tanks. Returned at 2.45 pm. After lunch to see C.R.E. re water supply & he lent me a tracing of ditto. At 6.30 pm to see ADMS with water map which he kept. Left his office 7.50 pm. Trench maps lent to me.	E.J.H.
		P.M. 8.0	To "café" to dinner with Sproat. Weather, Showery	

2449 Wt. W14957/M90 750,000 1/16 J.B.C. & A. Forms/C.2118/12.

Instructions regarding War Diaries and Intelligence Summaries are contained in F. S. Regs., Part II. and the Staff Manual respectively. Title Pages will be prepared in manuscript.

WAR DIARY
or
~~INTELLIGENCE~~ SUMMARY
(Erase heading not required.)

Army Form C. 2118.

Place	Date	Hour	Summary of Events and Information	Remarks and references to Appendices
	19-8-16	AM 6.0	At 6.15 as car had not arrived as arranged proceeded by 71st F. Amb. which car came up [illegible] as I was enquiring. With Corporal Cummins proceeded to [illegible] a conducted tour of inspection of water supply. Found part of system [illegible] but the remaining supplies were by wells & pumps. Reached 69th F. Amb. A.D.S. at 2 pm & after getting car at 71st F. Amb. A.D.S. arrived back [illegible] at 4.0 pm. Mr. [illegible] came in to report that he was leaving the Division; this will materially upset the work of the Section till new interpreter gets the "hang of things". Censored letters, paid personnel, correspondence, diary &c.	[illegible]
		P.M. 11.0	To see ADMS. He asked for report on A.D.S. [illegible] by tomorrow. I spoke re water supply [illegible], showing	
	20.8.16	AM 9.0	To try & find Water Officer. Found he belonged [illegible]. He came to office later with Corpl. Cummins. Sent for Ford Car from 71st F. Amb. They were unable to send one & [illegible] who [illegible] one to get one from 69th F. Amb. The car did not arrive for me till nearly one o'clock. [illegible] preliminary report on water supply. At 2.0 proceeded to [illegible] billet at [illegible] then [illegible] 71st A.D.S. & then with Staff Surg. to A.D.S. where I made notes for sanitation report, [illegible] 69th A.D.S. On return at 7 pm called at ADMS Office but ADMS was out. [illegible] report sanitation at A.D.S. & water report on water supply.	[illegible]
		P.M. 10.30	To see ADMS & handed him reports of sanitation A.D.S. & water. Spoke re [illegible] at billet just vacated by 71st A.D.S.	
	21.8.16	AM 9.0	Censored letters, cleaning up correspondence &c. Water officer came in & [illegible] brought plans [illegible] supply which he called again [illegible] plans [illegible]. To office of D.D.M.S. to enquire re latrine [illegible]. Diary &c. To see Staff Surg. at billet [illegible] proposed horse lines K.O.Y.L.I. [illegible] both these camps are being made. To R.E. dump [illegible] re type latrine. For the conference at 69th F. Amb. at [illegible] but on arrival was told it had been postponed. On return journey met [illegible] he gave me a lift. Getting out scheme for the area with [illegible].	[illegible]
		P.M. 10.30	Saw ADMS & discussed sanitation generally. He gave me letter re sending man to Water Tank Co. [illegible]	

2449 Wt. W14957/M90 750,000 1/16 J.B.C. & A. Forms/C.2118/12.

Army Form C. 2118.

Instructions regarding War Diaries and Intelligence Summaries are contained in F. S. Regs., Part II. and the Staff Manual respectively. Title Pages will be prepared in manuscript.

WAR DIARY
or
INTELLIGENCE SUMMARY
(Erase heading not required.)

Place	Date	Hour	Summary of Events and Information	Remarks and references to Appendices
	22/8/16	A.M. 9. 0	To see O.C. 11th F. Amb re occupying old A.D.S. to which he agreed, he could not let me have a car. To Pont d'Achelles with new interpreter (M. Goupil [illegible] division yesterday) to see new billet. Visited motor transport column to try [illegible] petrol tins. Returned to billet at 1 pm. Went on horseback. In afternoon answered letters (25) [illegible] getting out orders for placing of [illegible] getting out sketches of [illegible] &c. Diary.	
		P.M. 10.30	To see ADMS but only spoke re moving from Steenwerck to [illegible] [illegible]. [illegible]	E.J.M.
Steenwerck to near Pont d'Achelles	23/8/16	A.M. 9. 0	Office work. On horseback to [illegible] billet & supervising work. Visit [illegible] [illegible] M.G.C. camp & making arrangements to put camp in satisfactory condition. On way back met Capt Gill. To 11th F. Amb to arrange re [illegible] of [illegible] A.D.S. Moved to new billet. To Advanced billet to [illegible] [illegible]	E.J.M.
		P.M. 9. 0	Orders [illegible] [illegible]. [illegible]	
	24/8/16	A.M. 9. 0	Censored letters, diary &c. To billet to see constructional work for A.D.S. returned. [illegible] M.G.C. to [illegible] Capt [illegible] re work [illegible]. Visit M.O. i/c 102 R.F.A. [illegible] A. Bill [illegible] [illegible] to see wagon lines of [illegible] Bdes. [illegible] required construction, [illegible] [illegible] not [illegible]. In evening [illegible] A.D.M.S. nothing on [illegible]. [illegible]	E.J.M.
		P.M. 9.30	[illegible] N.C.O.s &c. [illegible]	
	25/8/16	A.M. 9. 0	Received instructions at about 11.30 pm last night [illegible]. Office [illegible] morning. Correspondence, censoring letters, diary &c. To inspect works in progress at 102 [illegible] [illegible] M.G.C. With [illegible] [illegible] to investigate [illegible] case of [illegible]. [illegible] afternoon. Arranged for [illegible] of [illegible]. To see O.C. [illegible] [illegible] [illegible] [illegible]. To see O.C. [illegible] F. Amb [illegible] re [illegible] at Ambulance [illegible] [illegible] [illegible].	E.J.M.
		P.M. 8. 0	Received [illegible] from O.C. 11th [illegible] Field Ambulance [illegible] Office work [illegible] for [illegible] morning. [illegible]	
	26/8/16	A.M. 9. 0	Office work. [illegible] for [illegible]. [illegible] [illegible] Capt [illegible]. [illegible] In afternoon to [illegible] & arranged re [illegible]. [illegible] to inspect works at [illegible] M.G.C. [illegible] 102 R.F.A. wagon lines. Arranged with [illegible] re [illegible]. [illegible] M.C.O.s correspondence &c. Met Capt Gill [illegible] [illegible] M.G.C.	E.J.M.
		P.M. 9. 30	[illegible]	

2449 Wt. W14957/M90 750,000 1/16 J.B.C. & A. Forms/C.2118/12.

Instructions regarding War Diaries and Intelligence Summaries are contained in F. S. Regs., Part II. and the Staff Manual respectively. Title Pages will be prepared in manuscript.

Army Form C. 2118.

WAR DIARY
or
INTELLIGENCE SUMMARY

(Erase heading not required.)

Place	Date	Hour	Summary of Events and Information	Remarks and references to Appendices
	24.8.16	A.M. 9.0	The first anniversary of our landing in France. At present the Sanitary Section [illegible] of its original men, 21 RAMC 2 ASC, Evacuations 4 RAMC, (Cpl [illegible] with [illegible], [illegible] with ulcerated leg, Pte [illegible] [illegible], [illegible] transferred to [illegible] Co). At the moment section is very short as [illegible] are required for [illegible], [illegible], [illegible] at D125. [illegible] [illegible] from hospital. Cleaning up papers, [illegible]. To 71st F.A. A.D.S. [illegible] [illegible] or two alterations. To advanced billet [illegible] to [illegible] [illegible] complained of by M.O. [illegible] accumulation of [illegible]. Making drawing of standing orders for sanitation at personnel [illegible]. Weather fine	E.J.H.
		P.M. 11.0	To see ADMS & dined at "B" mess.	
	28.8.16	A.M. 9.0	Office work. To inspect [illegible] at 102 RFA. [illegible] also at K.O.Y.L.I. [illegible] which [illegible] course of construction. Also at Wagon Lines of D104 RFA. [illegible] A 103, 3 RFA [illegible] At Q.S. Staff, [illegible] B.103 RFA Wagon lines which were in a very unsanitary state. Report sent in re latter [illegible] 103 A. Received [illegible] from ADMS re [illegible]. Reports sent in re [illegible]. In evening met A.D.M.S. on horseback [illegible] "manure dump" report. Two [illegible].	E.J.H.
		P.M. 9.30	With Sgt. Elkington [illegible] manure dumps. Orders &c. Weather, fine.	
	29.9.16	A.M. 9.0	Diary, correspondence &c. Proceeded on horseback with Sgt. Elkington to select sites for manure dumps in the divisional area, both morning & afternoon. Go to advanced billet. Got drenched with rain in afternoon. Before setting out in afternoon saw ADMS who said permission was granted to me to have a [illegible].	E.J.H.
		P.M. 9.0	Orders, office work, N.C.Os reports &c. Weather, Very wet	
7 Cat reported for duty. Used in morning but not afternoon	30.9.16	A.M. 9.0	To 69th [illegible] & 70th Bde [illegible] to make arrangements re demonstration on the use of water carts. To 69th F. Amb. [illegible] to supply some material for the latrines of personnel. To A.D.S. 69th F.A. [illegible] Capt Woodhouse [illegible] re latrines. [illegible] & two sites for manure dumps. The A.D.M.S. looked in during afternoon [illegible] re demonstration on water carts. On report of suggestion [illegible] A.D.M.S. said [illegible] that evening.	E.J.H.
		P.M. 10.0	[illegible] manure dumps &c. N.C.Os reports, &c. Weather, fine at first. Rain later	

2449 Wt. W14957/M90 750,000 1/16 J.B.C. & A. Forms/C.2118/12.

Instructions regarding War Diaries and Intelligence Summaries are contained in F. S. Regs., Part II. and the Staff Manual respectively. Title Pages will be prepared in manuscript.

WAR DIARY
or
~~INTELLIGENCE SUMMARY~~

(Erase heading not required.)

Army Form C. 2118.

Place	Date	Hour	Summary of Events and Information	Remarks and references to Appendices
Y. Car used morning & afternoon	31.8.16	AM 9.0	Office work. On Ford car to Bergueneuse [illegible] S.S.O. office re Dickinson [illegible] wounded. [illegible] [illegible] inspected [illegible]. At A.P.M. office for new [illegible] [illegible] station. Saw D.A.D.O.S. [illegible] [illegible] of travelling [illegible]. Returned at 1.30 pm after [illegible] [illegible]. [illegible] In afternoon to M.O.s conference at HQrs of Corps [illegible] [illegible] cases, dental cases, bathing arrangements, sanitary conditions of [illegible] [illegible], care of [illegible] [illegible] cards. [illegible] gave a [illegible] [illegible] with [illegible] of [illegible] on the storage of spare parts [illegible]. To tea with HQrs F.A. Visited 17/102 Wagon [illegible] station 70th (now 68th) M.G.C. camp. Suggested improvements to Staff Capt who accompanied me.	[illegible]
		PM 10.0	Reports [illegible] [illegible] clerical work etc. Received [illegible] [illegible]. [illegible]	

2449 Wt. W14957/M90 750,000 1/16 J.B.C. & A. Forms/C.2118/12.

Sept. 1916

140/1754

CONFIDENTIAL

Vol 13

WAR DIARY

OF

O.C. 40th SANITARY SECTION

R.A.M.C.(T); 23rd Division.

(September 1916)

(Volume 13)

Instructions regarding War Diaries and Intelligence Summaries are contained in F. S. Regs., Part II. and the Staff Manual respectively. Title Pages will be prepared in manuscript.

Army Form C. 2118.

WAR DIARY
or
~~INTELLIGENCE SUMMARY~~
(Erase heading not required.)

Place	Date	Hour	Summary of Events and Information	Remarks and references to Appendices
(PLOEGSTEERT AREA) PONT D'ACHELLES	1-9-16	A.M. 8.45	Water report revision. Answering letters. Running orders. O.C. No 2 Section D.A.C. called re burial of horse. M.O. 9th S. Staffs called re supply of quicklime etc. Diary. To see new camp of 51st D.S.C. Arrangements being commenced. To 171st Tunnelling Co. to see [illegible] for [illegible] but found them unsatisfactory for this purpose. In afternoon gave lecture on travelling kitchens, water carts etc at 40th Bde [illegible].	[illegible]
		P.M. 9.45	Discussing water supplies with Cpl Gunner. Also reports of Sgt Humphreys, Cpl Tudor [illegible] & [illegible] [illegible]. Weather fine, cold.	
	2.9.16	A.M. 8.45	Clearing up papers. TO BAILLEUL to draw money from Field Cashier. Saw Cpl. [illegible] [illegible] D.P.S. [illegible] a [illegible] for one. In afternoon O.C. San Sec. 19th Div. called & informed him of procedure [illegible] by this Section. To 69th Bde gave demonstration on travelling kitchens & water carts. Cpl Gunner reported re water supply at Ploegsteert Wood. [illegible] Weather fine.	[illegible]
		midnight	Gas alarm sounded but no result.	
	3.9.16	A.M. 6.30	With Corpl. Gunner to inspect water supply, Ploegsteert Wood. Found same most unsatisfactory after investigation. Returned at 2 p.m. Drawing up report thereon. To Erquinghem. Certain amount of damage done but not so much as report had stated.	[illegible]
		P.M. 10.0	On with reports, orders etc. In Ploegsteert Road inspected water cart of D 102 R.F.A. which was in a shocking condition. Weather fine.	
	4.9.16	A.M. 9.0	Answering letters, preparing reports etc. At 11.0 a.m. O.C. 19th Div. San. Sec. came & with him visited ADS of [illegible] F. Amb & camps at La Romarin, Oosthove farm, [illegible]. After lunch to see [illegible] officer in charge of water arrangements & also to [illegible] of lower [illegible] via La Romarin back.	[illegible]
		P.M. 10.0	Completing reports, working through papers. Weather Showery.	

2449 Wt. W14957/M90 750,000 1/16 J.B.C. & A. Forms/C.2118/12.

Instructions regarding War Diaries and Intelligence Summaries are contained in F. S. Regs., Part II. and the Staff Manual respectively. Title Pages will be prepared in manuscript.

WAR DIARY
or
~~INTELLIGENCE SUMMARY~~
(Erase heading not required.)

Army Form C. 2118.

Place	Date	Hour	Summary of Events and Information	Remarks and references to Appendices
	5.9.16	A.M. 9.0	Office work. Set out walking with L/Cpl Smith for BAILLEUL, to inspect sanitary exhibition. To 7 Clothier (also saw A.D.M.S. when returning from there) in his office. Visited exhibition & instructed Smith to make sketches. Capt Bell accompanied me. Some of the exhibits are ingenious but a large number are impracticable in the field except with an RAMC or stationary unit. Infantry battalions are the difficult units to deal with. Arrived back at 2 p.m. In later part of afternoon visited D.A.C. with M.O. Sections	[illegible]
		P.M. 11.0	1, 2 & 3. Sent M.O. written report. Clearing up office work also arrangements for move. Weather: Raining all day.	
PONT D'ACHELLES (PLOEGSTEERT AREA) TO TILQUES	6.9.16	A.M. 6.30	To inspect men's billet. By road to BAILLEUL to entrain. Party (2nd) had left in lorries. Entrained 8.30 a.m. Arrived S'OMER 11 a.m. Marched to TILQUES, arrived 1 p.m. Lorry of Foden Steam Lorry Disinfector (attached 2 days ago) did not arrive till 5.15 p.m. Foden lorry [illegible] moved slowly. At 6 p.m. with Sergt Elkington to inspect water supply at Generals billet & at RAMC messes & also at Headqrs. Met ADMS who spoke re camp ground & camps at WATTEN.	[illegible]
		P.M. 11.0	Saw A.D.M.S. 10.30 p.m. He instructed me to arrange re placing men out at Fd. Amb. also re water duty course for the water men. He said he would enquire what the duties of the water officer were. Weather: Fine	
	7.9.16	A.M. 8.30	Instructions & arrangements for work of section. Staff Sergt to inspect camps at WATTEN. Sergt Humphries + 2 men attached 71st F. Amb., Sergt Chapman + 2 men, 69th F. Amb., Cpl Tabor + 1 man 70th F. Amb. Remainder to stop at Headqrs. Cpl Hawker & 1 man on inspection, Cpl Dunn's water duty. [illegible] on D. [illegible] etc. Cpl Tribe on disinfector. To WATTEN to inspect reinforcement camp.	
		P.M. 9.0	Drawing up report, clerical work etc. Going through old papers for destroying of useless ones. ~~[illegible]~~ Weather: Fine	[illegible]

2449 Wt. W14957/M90 750,000 1/16 J.B.C. & A. Forms/C.2118/12.

Army Form C. 2118.

WAR DIARY
or
~~INTELLIGENCE SUMMARY~~

(Erase heading not required.)

Instructions regarding War Diaries and Intelligence Summaries are contained in F. S. Regs., Part II. and the Staff Manual respectively. Title Pages will be prepared in manuscript.

Place	Date	Hour	Summary of Events and Information	Remarks and references to Appendices
	8.9.16	A.M. 9.0	Getting particulars to-gether for water lecture. To 70th F. Amb at ETREHEM & gave lecture 10 am to 12 noon. Twelve men present. A.D.M.S. came up just after lecture terminated	
			In afternoon to MORBRUGGES to see disinfector at work at 11th M.R. Capt Tubb in charge. 365 kits were done by 11 am next day.	[illegible]
		—	Office work. Played in a little football match with the men. Weather fine	
	9.9.16	A.M. 9.0	Answering letters &c. To 70th F Amb & gave second lecture on water duties.	
			Bathing parade. Arrangements for move to-morrow. Two [illegible] arrived from P. C. of [illegible]	[illegible]
			To see ADMS at 10 pm but no special instructions.	
		—	Owing to move men [illegible] not returned to unit [illegible] evening. Weather fine.	
TILQUES TO ~~[illegible]~~ ALLONVILLE	10.9.16	A.M. 6.30	Preparations for move. Orderly room. Sgt. Humphries & Cpl Hawkins up on charge of drunkenness.	[illegible]
			Left in lorry at 9.30 via S^T OMIER - AIRE - DOULLENS - TALMAS. [illegible]	
			Arrived destination at 6.30 pm after a tolerably comfortable journey.	
			To dinner with Capt Gill at C mess. No billet available for me so turned in to a barn. Weather fine	
	11.9.16	A.M. 8.45	Section under S/Cpl Sproul arrived at billet at 8 am. Staff(C) [illegible] to [illegible] Hospital at S^T OMIER was detained. Cpl Tubb & Pte Drake at orderly room on charge of drunkenness & absence from billets.	[illegible]
		P.M. 10.0	Office work. Inspected village of ALLONVILLE & found it in very [illegible] condition. Submitted report. Saw ADMS [illegible] & [illegible] for map of sanitation area with Capt Gill. Weather fine	
ALLONVILLE TO BAIZIEUX	12.9.16	A.M. 9.0	Section moved from ALLONVILLE to BAIZIEUX, with [illegible] group. I followed later on horseback via S^T GRATIEN to see re lorry at A.S.C. for new spring.	
			Looking for billets for section. A.D.M.S. said he wished me to carry on a complete water duty lecture for 68th Inf Bde before carrying on with scheme. Phoned Staff Captains of these brigades & made arrangements.	[illegible]
		P.M. 11.0	Weather fine.	

2449 Wt. W14957/M90 750,000 1/16 J.B.C. & A. Forms/C.2118/12.

Instructions regarding War Diaries and Intelligence Summaries are contained in F. S. Regs., Part II. and the Staff Manual respectively. Title Pages will be prepared in manuscript.

WAR DIARY
or
INTELLIGENCE SUMMARY
(Erase heading not required.)

Army Form C. 2118.

Place	Date	Hour	Summary of Events and Information	Remarks and references to Appendices
	13.9.16	A.M. 9.0	Detailing personnel for work. To HENENCOURT WOOD to lecture on water duties to 69th Bde. In evening [illegible] again. To see ADMS in evening re approval for 68th Bde to have use of [illegible] Disinfector for four days.	EJM
		P.M. 10.30	Weather: Dull	
	14.9.16	A.M. 9.0	To MILLENCOURT to give lecture on water duties to 68th Bde. On return in afternoon attended MO's conference at ADMS office. Office work. Saw ADMS. Letter for use of lorry from 69th Inf. Bde	EJM
	15.9.16	A.M. 9.0	With Sergt. Chapman inspected HENENCOURT. Saw Corps Camp Commandant. In afternoon with Cpl. Summers to MILLENCOURT (also Lt. SPRIAT) inspected village. Saw T. Major & arranged to finish inspection with him tomorrow. Saw ADMS in evening who instructed me to visit BRESLE to select latrine sites. Baths returned owing to lorry not getting load of clothing from 68th Bde as arranged. To see Col. Walk[illegible] re same.	EJM
		P.M. 11.0	Weather: Fine	
	16.9.16	A.M. 9.0	To draw money at D.H.Q. To BRESLE with Sergt. [illegible] to choose sites for latrines. Saw [illegible] re spraying of the mess [illegible]. CRE inspected and [illegible]. Promised & carried out [illegible]. Saw Corporal of 1st Div. San. Sec. Also at BRESLE in afternoon carrying on inspection. [illegible] BRESLE, CONTAY, & MONTIGNY. [illegible] saw Col Walk[illegible] In evening saw ADMS re overlapping at BRESLE, CONTAY, [illegible] re same.	EJM
		P.M. 10.0	Weather: Fine	
	17.9.16	A.M. 9.0	Paid men. To MILLENCOURT to complete inspection of village. Met Cpl Summers there with T. Major. In afternoon wrote letters & office work. Football match [illegible] Sanitary S. v. [illegible] [illegible]. Saw ADMS in evening [illegible] re overlapping of areas.	EJM
		P.M. 10.0	Clearing up some papers at office. Weather: Fine at first, dull later	

2449 Wt. W14957/M90 750,000 1/16 J.B.C. & A. Forms/C.2118/12.

Instructions regarding War Diaries and Intelligence Summaries are contained in F. S. Regs., Part II. and the Staff Manual respectively. Title Pages will be prepared in manuscript.

WAR DIARY
or
~~INTELLIGENCE SUMMARY~~
(Erase heading not required.)

Army Form C. 2118.

Place	Date	Hour	Summary of Events and Information	Remarks and references to Appendices
	18.9.16	A.M. 9.0	With Cpl. [illegible] taken to BAVELINCOURT & BEAUCOURT to inspect villages. Saw officers of [illegible] & [illegible] on T. Majors. Heavy rain. In afternoon on office work. Diary has not been written daily since 11th inst & it was difficult matter to recall details. Did not report to ADMS to-day but received note from Capt Bell making appointment to meet ADMS at 9 a.m. to-morrow to inspect villages. Weather Wet all day.	[illegible]
	19.9.16	A.M. 9.0	To meet ADMS with him & Capt Bell on horseback to D.R.S. at BAIZIEUX to see O.C. 1st Northumbrian Amb re T.U. men for sanitary work. To 40th F. Amb. encampment. At BRESLE, HENENCOURT & MILLENCOURT saw T. Majors at the first [illegible] villages. In afternoon with Sergt. [illegible] to inspect BAIZIEUX. Met ADMS 15th Div. Looked round wood & found a number of what were covered pits but which were now nothing better than open pits. Lorry left this morning to draw rations at Q.[illegible] & did not return till 6.30 p.m. ADMS sent chit re why his material had not arrived. Weather Showery.	[illegible]
		P.M. 9.0	Correspondence &c	
	20.9.16	A.M. 9.0	Clearing up letters, diary, notes &c. To MONTIGNY saw Capt [illegible] O.C. 1st Div San Sec. Arranged re BRESLE supervision which he undertook to do same. In afternoon saw O.C. 40th F. Amb. re rations in consequence of ADMS note. To Divl. Headqrs. Inspected same [illegible] open pits being closed. [illegible] saw Capt Bell & also A.D.M.S. explained re delay re supervision of rations. Returned at 4 p.m. Weather Wet.	[illegible]
		P.M. 11.0	Arrangements for work &c. So much detail has to be arranged for.	
	21.9.16	A.M. 9.0	Party of 18 L.D. men turned up as per verbal message from 40 DRS. To HENENCOURT WOOD. Saw T. Major & with Sgt. Chapman inspected wood encampments. 41st Div. Bde coming in. To BAIZIEUX WOOD inspected same with Sergt. [illegible]. Many latrines [illegible]. Capt Cole arrived as a reinforcement.	[illegible]
		P.M. 10.30	Correspondence &c. Weather Fine	

Army Form C. 2118.

Instructions regarding War Diaries and Intelligence Summaries are contained in F. S. Regs., Part II. and the Staff Manual respectively. Title Pages will be prepared in manuscript.

WAR DIARY
or
INTELLIGENCE SUMMARY

(Erase heading not required.)

Place	Date	Hour	Summary of Events and Information	Remarks and references to Appendices
	22.9.16	A.M. 9.0	Censoring letters etc. To MONTIGNY & called at 1st Div. S.O. office but he was out. On to CHATEAU [illegible] BEAUCOURT met Cpl Tabor [illegible] Corpl Hawker & spoke re water points. Met T. Major & [illegible] [illegible] [illegible] inspected an unsanitary house. On to CONTAY with Corp. Hawker. In afternoon to HENENCOURT WOOD saw Sgt Chapman. Camp – a dirty state as reported by [illegible]. Staff Capt. not available but saw another officer reported to him. Sent letter later. To [illegible] Div Supply dump re [illegible]	[initials]
		P.M. 10.0	Office work. 31st L.U. men reported for duty from D.R.S. [signature]	
	23.9.16	A.M. 9.0	To BRESLE WOOD & [illegible] re water point. On with inspection of BAIZIEUX for sanitation scheme, with Sgt Elkington. In evening saw T. Major [illegible] him [illegible] manure dump etc. Drawing up	[initials]
		P.M. 10.0	scheme. A.D.M.S called in afternoon but I was out. Drawing up BAIZIEUX scheme [signature]	
	24.9.16	A.M. 9.0	To HENENCOURT WOOD saw Sgt Chapman, [illegible] for [illegible] being dug. On to MILLENCOURT saw Staff C[apt] [illegible] Cpl [illegible] re scheme of latrines. In afternoon making tracing of MILLENCOURT. Capt Bell arrived to [illegible] [illegible] [illegible] [illegible] T.U. men	[initials]
			Censoring letters, diary, correspondence etc. Heard news of Col. Walker's death. [signature]	
	25.9.16	AM 9.0	To Town Major's re cart for refuse [illegible] another cart found by Interpreter. To [illegible] [illegible] on horse [illegible] camp. Lunch at 'C' mess. In afternoon went round boundary of area with Sgt Humphreys, inspected some of the camps. Returned to office at 6.15 pm. To inspect latrines just erected [illegible] in [illegible]. Received [illegible] for [illegible]	[initials]
		P.M. 10.45	Office work & section arrangements. ADMS spoke re [illegible] at water points & also that [illegible] on D.D.M.S. [illegible] [signature]	
	26.9.16	A.M. 9.0	Censoring letters, circulars etc. To HENENCOURT WOOD. On to HENENCOURT [illegible] at DDMS office & also APM (Corps) but matter [illegible] Called at 47th Div. ADMS but he was out. Saw DADMS. In afternoon to MILLENCOURT to complete latrine scheme. Inspected work	[initials]
		P.M. 9.0	[illegible]. Correspondence etc. [signature]	

2449 Wt. W14957/M90 750,000 1/16 J.B.C. & A. Forms/C.2118/12.

Army Form C. 2118.

WAR DIARY
or
INTELLIGENCE SUMMARY

(Erase heading not required.)

Instructions regarding War Diaries and Intelligence Summaries are contained in F. S. Regs., Part II. and the Staff Manual respectively. Title Pages will be prepared in manuscript.

Place	Date	Hour	Summary of Events and Information	Remarks and references to Appendices
	27.9.16	A.M. 9.0	Office work, report on BAIZIEUX etc. Reclaim to water duty men attending for instruction. In afternoon to MILLENCOURT & inspected work in progress & to HENENCOURT [illegible] Chapman.	
		P.M. 9.0	On with sanitation schemes etc. [illegible]	[illegible]
	28.9.16	A.M. 9.0	Office work. Instruction to water duty men: To see Town Major BAIZIEUX re [illegible] for report. ADMS called at office.	
		P.M. 10.0	In afternoon to MONTIGNY [illegible] Capt [illegible] 1st Div also BEAUCOURT [illegible] camp [illegible]. Censoring, correspondence on [illegible] reported. [illegible]	[illegible]
	29.9.16	A.M. 9.0	To A.A. Co & R.F.C. Squadron on HENENCOURT [illegible] camps, the latter with M.O. to On to MILLENCOURT inspected work in progress, incinerators being built, also sites of proposed camp [illegible] places for latrines. In afternoon attended III Corps DDMS conference. On return with Staff Capt. 15th Div [illegible] Capt 45 Inf Bde to select sites for latrines at Bde camps about to be put up at BAIZIEUX. [illegible]	[illegible]
		P.M. 9.0	Clerical work	
	30.9.16	A.M. 9.0	To see re workshop for [illegible]. Inspected new latrines near T. Majors office message from ADMS 1st Div. Saw [illegible] DADMS inspected [illegible] area. Setting out sites of latrines of camps at BAIZIEUX of 45th Bde. Censoring letters clerical work etc. T. Major of HENENCOURT WOOD came [illegible] T. Major BAIZIEUX called re [illegible] [illegible] to inspect BAISLE WOOD but it became too dark [illegible]. DADMS 16th Div called re latrines at [illegible] camps	[illegible]
		A.M. 10.30	BAIZIEUX [illegible] Office work [illegible] [illegible]	

2449 Wt. W14957/M90 750,000 1/16 J.B.C. & A. Forms/C.2118/12.

Oct. 1916

140/1811

23
Vol 14

CONFIDENTIAL.

WAR DIARY OF THE

40th SANITARY SECTION, R.A.M.C. (T) 23rd Div

(from October 1st to October 31st 1916).

(Volume 14).

Instructions regarding War Diaries and Intelligence Summaries are contained in F. S. Regs., Part II. and the Staff Manual respectively. Title Pages will be prepared in manuscript.

WAR DIARY
or
INTELLIGENCE SUMMARY
(Erase heading not required.)

Army Form C. 2118.

Place	Date	Hour	Summary of Events and Information	Remarks and references to Appendices
BAIZIEUX	1·10·16	A.M. 9.0	Time last night put back one hour. [illegible] letters, correspondence &c. To water point at BAIZIEUX & [illegible] duty man re keeping note book properly. By car to HENENCOURT. Inspected A.S.C. (4th) camp & [illegible] — the adoption of [illegible] latrines. At WOOD [illegible] duty man [illegible] on [illegible]. To HENENCOURT. Saw III Corps D.D.M.S. for a moment. [illegible] III Corps & [illegible] for ambulance & lorry. To Field Cashier for money. Saw Lt. Chapman on [illegible]. In afternoon on office work. D.A.D.M.S. 1st Div. called but told him [illegible] for latrines [illegible] not yet [illegible] material. Saw R.E. officer from III Corps who called re [illegible] of latrines at BAIZIEUX. [illegible] Capt. [illegible] [illegible] he could not come. L/Cpl. Smith returned with [illegible] about 15 [illegible].	[initials]
		A.M. 9.0	[illegible] inspected latrines in [illegible] with Staff Capt. & Lt. Chapman. Paid [illegible]. T. Major BAIZIEUX called re sanitary orders. On with diary, correspondence, [illegible] &c. Weather fine	
	2.10.16	A.M. 9.0	Inspecting constructional work at workshops. To BRESLE WOOD inspected area, [illegible] of food refuse about but no unit in occupation. Also 1st Div. [illegible] on [illegible]. In afternoon to [illegible] (Div.) camp & met Capt. [illegible] on the road. To CONTALMAISON to see ADMS [illegible]. Lost way on journey back, arriving BAIZIEUX about 8 pm.	[initials]
		P.M. 10.0	Correspondence &c. Weather, Rain all day	
	3.10.16	A.M. 9.0	At workshop. Inspected [illegible] ground. Staff Capt. 15th Div. called re progress of work on [illegible] accounts, letters &c. In afternoon to HENENCOURT & with Town Major visited [illegible] & inspected work in square. Not feeling well & returned at 4.15 pm. Received [illegible] from A.D.M.S. to send lorry [illegible]. T. Major came [illegible] to report re complaint [illegible]. Weather, Wet. After [illegible] Staff Capt. [illegible] Bde. re latrines for [illegible] at BAIZIEUX.	[initials]

2449 Wt. W14957/M90 750,000 1/16 J.B.C. & A. Forms/C.2118/12.

Army Form C. 2118.

Instructions regarding War Diaries and Intelligence Summaries are contained in F. S. Regs., Part II. and the Staff Manual respectively. Title Pages will be prepared in manuscript.

WAR DIARY

or

~~INTELLIGENCE SUMMARY~~

(Erase heading not required.)

Place	Date	Hour	Summary of Events and Information	Remarks and references to Appendices
	4-10-16	a.m. 9.0	[illegible] village. At 2.15 [illegible] A.D.M.S. office [illegible] T.U. men. [illegible] MILLENCOURT [illegible]	[illegible]
		p.m. 10.0	G.S. wagon did not [illegible] till 12.30 a.m. [illegible]	
	5.10.16	a.m. 9.0	[illegible] To MILLENCOURT. [illegible] A.D.M.S. [illegible] BAIZIEUX & HENENCOURT [illegible] T.U. [illegible] Staff Captain [illegible] BAIZIEUX [illegible]	[illegible]
		p.m. 9.20	2 & 3 [illegible]	
	6.10.16	a.m. 9.0	[illegible] RFA [illegible] HENENCOURT WOOD 50th Div. 151st Bde. [illegible] Staff Captain [illegible] BAIZIEUX [illegible]	[illegible]
		p.m. 9.15	[illegible]	

2449 Wt. W14957/M90 750,000 1/16 J.B.C. & A. Forms/C.2118/12.

Army Form C. 2118.

WAR DIARY
or
INTELLIGENCE SUMMARY

(Erase heading not required.)

Instructions regarding War Diaries and Intelligence Summaries are contained in F. S. Regs., Part II. and the Staff Manual respectively. Title Pages will be prepared in manuscript.

Place	Date	Hour	Summary of Events and Information	Remarks and references to Appendices
	7/10/16	a.m. 9.0	Correspondence &c. To HENENCOURT WOOD with Sergt Ellingham [illegible] measured latrines for superstructure. To see transport camp & [illegible]. Saw Town Major re P.B. men. Took nominal roll of these men. In afternoon to MILLENCOURT. Inspected work in progress at camps. Also with interpreter to try investigate ? diarrhoea among civilians. Many attributed it to bread. Saw Town Major & he handed me nominal roll of P.B. men. Four of these men are in hospital. On return found Capt Rayner at my billet, & had tea with him. To try & find guard room to put two P.B. prisoners in but battalions of [illegible] Div. not in yet.	
		P.M. 10.30	Office work, diary &c. T. Major of BAIZIEUX notified me re 100 biscuit boxes arriving. Weather, Windy [illegible]	
	8/10/16	a.m. 9.0	At 12.50 a.m. wire from ADMS to return Ford Ambulances. Office work &c. At 9.30 a.m. Capt Rayner came round & I inspected workshops &c with him in BAIZIEUX. To Town Major to see re biscuit boxes which Capt Nicholson said were not now available. Rayner came to lunch & during afternoon we discussed re sanitary matters &c. Lt. Wilson came with chit saying he was to take over area from me but as I had received no instructions told him to come tomorrow at 9.30 a.m. Getting out reports &c. Town Major & Lt Digby came to dinner. Weather, Rain	
BAIZIEUX to MONTIGNY	9/10/16	a.m. 8.30	Received instructions by Capt Smith at 11.30 p.m. last night re move. Arrangements for move. Lt A.C. Wilson 1st Northumbrian F. Amb came to take over. Getting out notes on work of Section in area &c. all the morning. Lorry returned from ADMS at about 11 a.m. It went for rations but returned as they were not to be drawn till afternoon. First load of equipment & personnel moved off at 3 p.m. to MONTIGNY. Inspected clearing up of billet. Left on my horse at 4.15 p.m. The former arrived at MONTIGNY at 5 p.m. The lorry at 9 p.m. Instructions re cleaning up kit equipment to Staff Sergt.	
		a.m. 9.45	Saw Capt Bell about 6 p.m. on my arrival. ADMS had had staff [illegible] [illegible]. No instructions. Saw Staff Sergt 15th Div San. Sect. Weather, Fine	

2449 Wt. W14957/M90 750,000 1/16 J.B.C. & A. Forms/C.2118/12.

Instructions regarding War Diaries and Intelligence Summaries are contained in F. S. Regs., Part II. and the Staff Manual respectively. Title Pages will be prepared in manuscript.

WAR DIARY
or
~~INTELLIGENCE SUMMARY~~

(Erase heading not required.)

Army Form C. 2118.

Place	Date	Hour	Summary of Events and Information	Remarks and references to Appendices
MONTIGNY	10/10/16	am 9.0	Inspected personnel at work cleaning equipment. Driving [illegible] &c. A Special Gas Officer arrived at 10.30 am. Office work, correspondence &c. Got with report on work done in "A" area. Kit inspection of men in afternoon. Capt [illegible] came just as I completed inspection. Tea with "C" Mess. ADMS away. ADMS sent for me & read draft report on disinfecting precautions [illegible]. Weather fine	EJM
	11/10/16	am 9.0	Inspected [illegible] with Sergt Etherington. Completed report on work done in area "A". Arrangements for tomorrow. Having to move no work of importance possible. Lorry loaded in afternoon. Nothing of importance to record. Weather fine	EJM
MONTIGNY to AILLY-LE-HAUT-CLOCHER	12/10/16	am 5.30	At 6 a.m. moved to ALBERT to entrain for LONGPRÉ. Train should have started at noon of [illegible] [illegible]. Journey very slow & did not arrive at LONGPRÉ till 4 a.m. — 13/10/16. Proceeded [illegible] by lorry to AILLY-LE-HAUT-CLOCHER. Weather fine	EJM
AILLY-LE-HAUT-CLOCHER to ST RIQUIER	13/10/16	am 5.0	Arrived at billet at 5 a.m. at AILLY. Section [illegible] & was moved on to ST RIQUIER at 11.30 a.m. Lorry leaving [illegible] at 8.30 a.m. & returned [illegible] [illegible]. [illegible] had fallen out [illegible] night but turned up during the afternoon. [illegible] to ST RIQUIER. Looking for billet & am billeted [illegible] in [illegible] area. Saw ADMS who asked for report on water supply & [illegible]. Weather fine	EJM
	14/10/16	am 9.0	Inspected town re water supply with Sergt Etherington, also Lt Robinson RAMC 71st FA [illegible] — report. Inspected town re sanitation — afternoon [illegible] some of the [illegible]. ADMS came to dinner. Weather fine	EJM

2449 Wt. W14957/M90 750,000 1/16 J.B.C. & A. Forms/C.2118/12.

Army Form C. 2118.

WAR DIARY
or
~~INTELLIGENCE SUMMARY~~

(Erase heading not required.)

Instructions regarding War Diaries and Intelligence Summaries are contained in F. S. Regs., Part II. and the Staff Manual respectively. Title Pages will be prepared in manuscript.

Place	Date	Hour	Summary of Events and Information	Remarks and references to Appendices
FROM ST RIQUIER TO POPERINGHE	15/10/16	AM 9 30	Office work [illegible] [illegible] letters & arrangements for move. In afternoon with ADMS to ABBEVILLE. To Field [illegible]. Section moved off at 10 pm for entrainment at CONTEVILLE. Accompanied by Salvage Co. C.R.E. was O.C. train. Arrived in good ~~[illegible]~~. Lorry left at 10 15 pm & proceeded by road. Health, [illegible]	[initials]
	16/10/16		Arrived at detraining station at HOUPOUTRE 8 30 am. Proceeded by road through POPERINGHE to Div Head Qrs camp where we were accomodated in tents. Lorry arrived at 4 30 pm having been awaiting at 2nd Australian Div. [illegible] [illegible] orderly. ~~[illegible]~~ Turned in early owing to lack of rest last night. Health fine	[initials]
	17/10/16	AM 9 0	Saw ADMS & received instructions to see Sanitary Off in 2nd Aust. Div. With Sgt Ellington to see S.O. 2nd Aus. Div. Obtained some particulars of the work & arranged to inspect [illegible] to morrow. On return received [illegible] from ADMS re sanitation in the trenches. Saw ADMS who asked me to draw up scheme. Submitted this to him in evening. Health fine	[initials]
		PM 9 30	Arranging for [illegible] and [illegible]. Office work &c.	
	18/10/16	AM 9 0	To see ADMS re trench scheme as he was unwell when I called last evening. He took same to the General but was approved. Arrived [illegible] at 2nd Aust. [illegible] [illegible] to meet S.O. with him to YPRES & inspected some of the area. In afternoon with Sgt Ellington to RE workshops re [illegible] for trench latrines.	[initials]
		PM 10.0	Showed same to ADMS in evening [illegible] [illegible] [illegible] to [illegible] away from RENINGHELST. ADMS [illegible] in [illegible] to-night. Health [illegible]	
	19/10/16	AM 9 0	To see Capt Gill re men to work at RE workshops, also saw Capt Baldwin & arranged re same. Answering letters & [illegible] correspondence &c. [illegible] from Field [illegible], [illegible] over to [illegible] & taking over from S.S. 2nd Aust. Div. to-morrow at [illegible]. On schemes of [illegible] for Divisional Area. Saw acting ADMS [illegible] [illegible] [illegible] [illegible] & SMO [illegible] [illegible] [illegible] [illegible] ADMS box. He said we must [illegible]. Health very well	[initials]

2449 Wt. W14957/M90 750,000 1/16 J.B.C. & A. Forms/C.2118/12.

Army Form C. 2118.

Instructions regarding War Diaries and Intelligence Summaries are contained in F. S. Regs., Part II. and the Staff Manual respectively. Title Pages will be prepared in manuscript.

WAR DIARY
or
INTELLIGENCE SUMMARY
(Erase heading not required.)

Place	Date	Hour	Summary of Events and Information	Remarks and references to Appendices
	20/10/16	a.m. 9.0	Moving to new encampment near POPERINGHE. Saw C.R.E. re work for latrines. Had touch of lumbago. Went with Sergt [illegible] to see Town Major at POPERINGHE, who informed me there was a Sanitary Officer for the town but he was out. On return met DADOS & spoke re lamps for office. Saw Capt Brummell at billets. Also Interpreter Carmier called & said no infectious cases at P. In afternoon on lorry & saw mobile section billet. Also CRE building party [illegible] of work. Instructions to Cpl Emmens re [illegible] particulars. Correspondence, diary etc. Took over billets from 1st San Sec. 2nd Australian Division to-day. Weather fine cool	[illegible]
	21/10/16	a.m. 9.0	Instructions to A/Cpl Smith re plans. Visited water points 64 & 11 tanks at POPERINGHE. Saw Australian Water Officer (Major) who gave me a plan of the sources. Met lorry returned on it to billet. In afternoon inspected camp of 16th D.A.C. 3rd Section just moved in. Also water point N.24. Cpl Emmens reported re water point. Received chit to ground to see Acting ADMS at headqrs. Reported to him the [illegible] General had complained re unsanitary state of billets at YPRES etc. etc. Diary, correspondence. Weather fine cool	[illegible]
	22/10/16	a.m. 9.0	Waiting for ambulance car promised for 9 a.m. Sent A/Cpl Smith at 10 o'clock to enquire. Car arrived 10.45. Proceeded with Sergt Chapman to YPRES [illegible] inspected the Hospice Infantry & Cavalry Barracks etc. On to the BUND inspected dug outs [illegible] Cpl Robinson & Cpl Hubbard. Saw O.C. [illegible] also M.O. [illegible] Returned at [illegible] & spoke Staff Captain 7th Bde re a [illegible] Returned billet arriving 6.15 pm. Found Sergt [illegible] instruction to Sergt Chapman re work [illegible] DDS saw Capt [illegible] to move with 17th F. Amb. [illegible] Office work, correspondence &c. Weather fine cool	[illegible]
	23/10/16	a.m. 9.0	Inspected own camp & found same required cleaning up. Set 2 men at work on same. Acting ADMS came & discussion with plans re YPRES, cavalry barracks etc. [illegible] To POPERINGHE & inspected billets of 11th W. Yorks & the 9th Yorks. Saw M.O.s in each case. In afternoon to Div. Laundry camp inspected same with A/Cpl Emmens. Capt [illegible] Answering letters, correspondence &c. Owing to no ambulance being available it is more or less impossible to inspect. Weather fine cool	[illegible]

2449 Wt. W14957/M90 750,000 1/16 J.B.C. & A. Forms/C.2118/12.

Army Form C. 2118.

WAR DIARY
or
INTELLIGENCE SUMMARY

(Erase heading not required.)

Instructions regarding War Diaries and Intelligence Summaries are contained in F. S. Regs., Part II. and the Staff Manual respectively. Title Pages will be prepared in manuscript.

Place	Date	Hour	Summary of Events and Information	Remarks and references to Appendices
	24/10/16	9.0 a.m.	[illegible] Field Ambulances. [illegible] A.P.M. [illegible]	[illegible]
	25/10/16	9.0 a.m.	[illegible] YPRES [illegible] 3 R.A.M.C. [illegible] At YPRES [illegible] RENINGHELST.	[illegible]

2449 Wt. W14957/M90 750,000 1/16 J.B.C. & A. Forms/C.2118/12.

Army Form C. 2118.

WAR DIARY
or
INTELLIGENCE SUMMARY
(Erase heading not required.)

Instructions regarding War Diaries and Intelligence Summaries are contained in F. S. Regs., Part II. and the Staff Manual respectively. Title Pages will be prepared in manuscript.

Place	Date	Hour	Summary of Events and Information	Remarks and references to Appendices
	26/10/16	AM 9.0	Getting out rough sketch of infantry barracks YPRES for report. To [illegible] to meet ADM. With ADMS discussing re sanitation at YPRES. With ADM inspected [illegible] at REMMGHE[illegible]. In afternoon clearing up correspondence. Dr. Walés reported. Diary, answering letters &c. Weather, fine [illegible]	[illegible]
	27/10/16	AM 9.0	No ambulance car came as written for. I called for same till 11 a.m. [illegible] with T.A.B. at 70th F Amb. Inspected camp just vacated by [illegible] Camp. At [illegible] inspected latrines &c. [illegible] [illegible] of F. Amb. [illegible] Ambulance. Obtained [illegible] Ambulance & visited the [illegible] divisional area with Capt. [illegible]. Called at RE [illegible]. [illegible] ready. Answering letters, diary, correspondence &c. Weather, fine	[illegible]
	28/10/16	AM 9.0	On horseback to inspect premises of civilian case of typhoid. To Salvage Co's billet but O.C. was out. At [illegible] Bde M.G.C. transport instructed them that they must burn excreta. To [illegible] billet. In afternoon to [illegible] inspected camps of 9th [illegible] Staffs [illegible], Labour Batt. [illegible] Transport lines, & 102nd RE. Generally the camps were in fair condition. Correspondence, answering letters &c. Walés report sent in to ADMS. Weather, fair showers.	[illegible]
	29/10/16	—	Though promised a Field Ambulance at 9.15 a.m. it did not arrive. Sent to [illegible] of F. Amb at 10.30 to enquire about it & it arrived about 11 o'clock. To YPRES [illegible] Chapman who reported work was proceeding satisfactorily. On way called at the Asylum [illegible] Capt [illegible] inspected ADS with him. It is [illegible] occupied by 57th Div. Went to the BUMD [illegible] Lt. [illegible] to ADS. With Capt [illegible] proceeded to ZILLEBEKE where I called at RAP & found MO to 8 KOYLI. With him went [illegible] trenches. The trenches were in a [illegible] condition, the latrines in a very bad state. Saw no reason why proposed sanitation scheme should not work. Met Capt [illegible] at the BUMD on the way back. Arrived at billet about 6.45 p.m. Office work. Weather, [illegible]	[illegible]

2449 Wt. W14957/M90 750,000 1/16 J.B.C. & A. Forms/C.2118/12.

Instructions regarding War Diaries and Intelligence Summaries are contained in F. S. Regs., Part II. and the Staff Manual respectively. Title Pages will be prepared in manuscript.

WAR DIARY
or
~~INTELLIGENCE SUMMARY~~

(Erase heading not required.)

Army Form C. 2118.

Place	Date	Hour	Summary of Events and Information	Remarks and references to Appendices
	30/10/16		Correspondence diary &c. [illegible] inspected [illegible] in area along Poperinghe. Reninghelst road [illegible] Post Office. [illegible] at camp of 191 C. A. [illegible] [illegible] In afternoon to POPERINGHE with M.O. [illegible] inspected billets. [illegible] building which appeared [illegible] improperly [illegible] [illegible] ADMS [illegible] [illegible] 2nd Army S.O. [illegible] at POPERINGHE [illegible] [illegible]	[illegible]
	31/10/16		Correspondence [illegible] ~~[illegible]~~ [illegible] In office all the morning, afternoon on getting up Sanitation notes &c. Salvage Officer called in afternoon. Office work. [illegible]	[illegible]

2449 Wt. W14957/M90 750,000 1/16 J.B.C. & A. Forms/C.2118/12.

Nov. 1916

Confidential

140/1862

Vol 15

WAR DIARY

of

O.C. 40th Sanitary Section R.A.M.C. T

23rd Division

(Volume 15)

Army Form C. 2118.

WAR DIARY
or
INTELLIGENCE SUMMARY

(Erase heading not required.)

Instructions regarding War Diaries and Intelligence Summaries are contained in F. S. Regs., Part II. and the Staff Manual respectively. Title Pages will be prepared in manuscript.

Place	Date	Hour	Summary of Events and Information	Remarks and references to Appendices
YPRES SALIENT. Nr POPERINGHE	1/11/16		No cart arrived as [illegible]. Proceeded on foot to [illegible] [illegible] inspected water [illegible] DIG. CASP. Met ADVS [illegible] lift as far as RE Dump. [illegible] [illegible] [illegible] [illegible] [illegible] inspected work. To BRULET [illegible] [illegible] [illegible]. [illegible] [illegible] [illegible] [illegible] afterwards [illegible] a [illegible] [illegible]. In afternoon to [illegible] [illegible]. Met O.C. [illegible] [illegible] on the way [illegible] experiments with chlorination treatment of [illegible] water. [illegible] ADMS [illegible] [illegible] [illegible] agreeable. Inspected [illegible] with Capt [illegible]. Reports etc. [illegible]	[illegible]
	2/11/16		Office work. At 10.30 am. to 69th F. Amb. [illegible] [illegible] [illegible] [illegible] to [illegible] for [illegible] [illegible] [illegible] ADMS [illegible]. To Town Major's office [illegible] Sanitary Officer [illegible] inspected billets of 8th KOYLI which were not quite satisfactory [illegible] [illegible] 11th H. [illegible] where [illegible] also [illegible] the M.O. [illegible] [illegible] [illegible] comparatively satisfactory, and also 2 companies of 8th [illegible] [illegible] which were satisfactory. In afternoon to [illegible] [illegible] [illegible] at [illegible]. Called at RE dump on way down [illegible] [illegible] [illegible] Capt [illegible] [illegible] ADMS [illegible]. Correspondence [illegible] [illegible] [illegible]	[illegible]
	3/11/16		Signed draft sanitary orders on [illegible] [illegible]. To POPERINGHE [illegible] [illegible] [illegible] against 11th H.F. Inspected [illegible] again [illegible] [illegible] M.O. [illegible] [illegible] [illegible] [illegible] up [illegible] [illegible] 11th H.F. To RENINGHELST [illegible] [illegible] [illegible] [illegible] [illegible] Clayton disinfector. The two ADMS's [illegible] [illegible] [illegible] [illegible] afternoon. On to [illegible] YPRES with [illegible] Smith. Saw Sergt Chapman [illegible] [illegible] (10th H.F.). Inspected billet with M.O. [illegible] [illegible] [illegible] [illegible] from [illegible] R.E. for [illegible] [illegible]. On to [illegible] [illegible] [illegible]. Returned with Sergt Chapman inspected [illegible] [illegible] [illegible] [illegible] [illegible] [illegible] barracks. Saw O.C. 10th W. Riding [illegible] [illegible]. Accounts, reports, censoring etc. [illegible] [illegible]	[illegible]

2449 Wt. W14957/M90 750,000 1/16 J.B.C. & A. Forms/C.2118/12.

Instructions regarding War Diaries and Intelligence Summaries are contained in F. S. Regs., Part II. and the Staff Manual respectively. Title Pages will be prepared in manuscript.

WAR DIARY
or
~~INTELLIGENCE~~ SUMMARY

(Erase heading not required.)

Army Form C. 2118.

Place	Date	Hour	Summary of Events and Information	Remarks and references to Appendices
	4.11.16		To inspect camps with Staff Sergt. inspected Winnipeg camp. Then with Sergt Humphries to Toronto camp, 40th Bde School of Instruction here. Met ADMS at KOYLI Transport lines. He mentioned re reports for visit of Surgeon General. In afternoon with Sergt Humphries inspected St LAWRENCE FERIE camps. Units in occupation were 10th & 40th M.G.C. Drawing up reports & maps for report. Weather fine	EJM
	5.11.16		Carrying on with inspection & reports on camps. At Montreal camp, also Winnipeg camp. On with reports. In evening to see ADMS with reports on Winnipeg & Toronto camps. He seemed well satisfied. Weather fine	EJM
	6.11.16		Visited all camps (St Lawrence Ferie, Toronto, Montreal & Winnipeg) to check a few details. Completed reports & plans of camps. Took same in to ADMS in the morning. To dinner with ADMS. Weather wet.	EJM
	7.11.16		Surgeon General visited camps about in the morning. The weather was terrible but inspection was completed. Rain continued all the afternoon. Office work. Weather v. wet	EJM
	8.11.16		Proceeded to the BVMD in connection with drawing up sanitary scheme, with Sergt [illegible]. Took Sergt Humphries to relieve Sergt Chapman. Met ADMS at the BVMD. He asked for a report on his memorandum re work of a Sanitary Section in the field. Drawing up report as instructed. Correspondence, [illegible] etc. Weather fine	EJM
	9.11.16		To RENINGHELST to see San. Officer 41st Div re Clayton machine. Inspected same but no more available. 10 of [illegible]. Correspondence, office work. In afternoon to M.O.'s conference at 40th F. Amb. Proceeded with ADMS to YPRES in connection with visit of DDMS. To Infantry Barracks, the Hospice & Eglise St Martin. Tea with ADMS. Office work. Weather fine	EJM

2449 Wt. W14957/M90 750,000 1/16 J.B.C. & A. Forms/C.2118/12.

Instructions regarding War Diaries and Intelligence Summaries are contained in F. S. Regs., Part II. and the Staff Manual respectively. Title Pages will be prepared in manuscript.

WAR DIARY
or
~~INTELLIGENCE SUMMARY~~
(Erase heading not required.)

Army Form C. 2118.

Place	Date	Hour	Summary of Events and Information	Remarks and references to Appendices
	10.11.16.		To the ASYLUM to meet ADMS. [illegible] ADMS [illegible] & we visited the Infantry Barracks, the Hospice & the Église St Martin. I then left them & proceeded to the RAMPARTS. Inspected billets of 64th MGC. Saw officers re same & gave advice. Met Sergt Humphreys. Inspected 40th T.M.B. Saw Staff Officer 40th Bde & made complaint as to filthy condition of billets. Saw MO i/c 180th RFA Bde who asked re water supplies. Inspecting for sites for ablution benches for ablution benches. To ASYLUM for food [illegible]. Paid Sergt Humphreys [illegible]. Saw Sanitary Officer of YPRES. Made arrangements for rationing, billeting & personnel who are to work on ablution benches at YPRES. Rev. Dobbs returned with me. In afternoon making sketches, taking out quantities & drawing up schemes for the BWMD [?]. Did not feel very well during evening. Correspondence, diary, etc.	
	11.11.16		To see X Corps Water Officer re various points: (1) Cleaning of tanks. He said he would arrange for [illegible] (2) Re complaints re chlorinating water at [illegible] Tanks (3) units will not be [illegible] on (4) [illegible] was arranged to [illegible] of water [illegible] [illegible] [illegible] [illegible] of water [illegible] [illegible] for sulphur [illegible] [illegible] along the POPERINGHE – [illegible] ROAD. [illegible] with the BWMD [illegible] In afternoon inspected 71st F. Amb. [illegible] [illegible] [illegible] [illegible] etc.	
	12.11.16.		To make enquiries of MOs 12th & 13th DLI re complaint as to no beds for [illegible] by MO 12th. Ascertained that they were [illegible] by the 12th which [illegible] the 13th at [illegible] [illegible]. To ADMS office to report [illegible]. In afternoon to YPRES. Met General who commented on unpleasant smell at RAMPARTS. Visited Inf. Barracks [illegible] with Sergt Humphreys. Saw [illegible] 40th [illegible] on the BWMD. Saw Dr Robinson MO 71st F. Amb. Office work, etc.	

2449 Wt. W14957/M90 750,000 1/16 J.B.C. & A. Forms/C.2118/12.

Army Form C. 2118.

WAR DIARY
or
~~INTELLIGENCE~~ SUMMARY

(Erase heading not required.)

Instructions regarding War Diaries and Intelligence Summaries are contained in F. S. Regs., Part II. and the Staff Manual respectively. Title Pages will be prepared in manuscript.

Place	Date	Hour	Summary of Events and Information	Remarks and references to Appendices
	13.11.16		Censoring letters &c. To POPERINGHE with Capt Bramwell concerned re experiments on [illegible] water treatment with chlorination. In afternoon to meet ARM representative but we missed each other. On to [illegible] again with L/Cpl PAMPOLO (who had returned from leave to day) & gave him instructions as to what was to be done. Compiling report of the BWMD sanitary scheme, correspondence &c. Weather fine	EJM
	14.11.16		Office work. To Sanitary Companies [illegible] Corps at 10th C.C.S. ADMS also informed. In afternoon inspecting [illegible] re manure dumps with Sergt Ellington [illegible] road from Town No 6 through YPRES - VLAMERTINGHE and to R.E. Dumps & obtained [illegible]. To see ADMS who mentioned [illegible] matters. Weather fine	EJM
	15/11/16		On with manure dumps inspection with Staff Sergt Ellington BUSSEBOOM - VLAMERTINGHE road in afternoon [illegible] [illegible] this morning. Was [illegible] with [illegible] this afternoon. Correspondence &c. Weather fine, cold	EJM
	16/11/16		Proceeded on foot with inspection of manure dumps. Also at 11th M.F. [illegible]. In afternoon on with manure disposal report. Not feeling very well. Saw Capt Chapman & Capt [illegible]. Censoring letters, diary, correspondence &c. Weather fine cold	EJM
	17/11/16		With Sergt Ellington inspecting of manure dumps on East side POPERINGHE - RENINGHELST Road also at [illegible] of [illegible]. Visited also MVS & 193 ASC Camp. In afternoon inspected manure dumps off OUDERDOM - VLAMERTINGHE ROAD with Sergt Ellington on the 71st F. Amb & the transport lines. To see ADMS but nothing of importance to report. Weather fine, v. cold	EJM

2449 Wt. W14957/M90 750,000 1/16 J.B.C. & A. Forms/C.2118/12.

Instructions regarding War Diaries and Intelligence Summaries are contained in F. S. Regs., Part II. and the Staff Manual respectively. Title pages will be prepared in manuscript.

WAR DIARY
or
~~INTELLIGENCE SUMMARY.~~
(Erase heading not required.)

Army Form C. 2118.

Place	Date	Hour	Summary of Events and Information	Remarks and references to Appendices
	18/11/16		Continued manure dumps inspection of 68th M.G.C. &c. Met ADMS who made arrangements to inspect water tanks tomorrow. Proceeded to Div Headqrs re manure disposal. In afternoon to 41st F Amb. transport lines but could not find 69th M.G.C. Saw the F Ambce at ABEELE. Completed report of manure disposal. Office work, correspondence &c. Weather fine.	[illegible]
	19/11/16		Met ADMS at 10 am & proceeded on inspection of the water tanks in the div. area. In afternoon to Div Headqrs to see L/Cpl Dand re clearing drawers &c. At R.E. dump & picked up Pte Povey & also some material for YPRES. To YPRES with Sgt Humphries inspected ablution bench being ~~constructed~~ & also re erection of latrine at the CLOISTERS. The bench at the RAMPARTS seems to be progressing rather slowly but Sgt Humphries had made a good show at cleaning the Bde Headqrs at the RAMPARTS. Cpl Brown knocked over by horse & shoulder dislocated. L/Cpl Smith proceeded on leave. This has made four matters rather disarranged. Correspondence, office work &c. Weather, fine.	~~[illegible]~~ [illegible]
20th all next sheet ←	21/11/16		Censoring letters, diary &c. To S.O. conference at No 10 C.C.S. but on arrival found it was cancelled. To 40th Bde School with L/Cpl Penfold & on to 10th M.F. transport re sanitary report. Met ADMS when returning from C.C.S. In afternoon to YPRES. Inspected ablution bench & also to Infantry Barracks saw M.O. 11th M.F. Inspected latrines, foot wash room &c. Saw Cpl Tabor. Correspondence &c. Weather fine cold.	[illegible]

2353 Wt. W2544/1454 700,000 5/15 D. D. & L. A.D.S.S./Forms/C. 2118.

Instructions regarding War Diaries and Intelligence Summaries are contained in F. S. Regs., Part II. and the Staff Manual respectively. Title pages will be prepared in manuscript.

WAR DIARY
or
~~INTELLIGENCE SUMMARY.~~
(Erase heading not required.)

Army Form C. 2118.

Place	Date	Hour	Summary of Events and Information	Remarks and references to Appendices
	20/11/16		Correspondence &c. To 68th M.G.C. inspected camp with transport officer during afternoon. At Baths during morning on investigations of chloride of lime treatment of water with Gen. with notes &c. Weather, fine, cold	E.F.M.
	22/11/16		At Baths all the morning on investigations re chloride of lime treatment of water. In afternoon clearing up office work. Getting out plan of a drying shed, latrine &c. Sent out receptacles to 41st Amb. Office work &c. Weather, fine	E.F.M.
	23/11/16		To Field Bakery inspected ovens at ... To YMCA Vaux Hall & made complaint to leader about condition of latrines &c. To 40th Bde School & saw latrines being erected. To RE dump re material. Paid men. In afternoon to the Asylum YPRES to conference. Discussion on infectious jaundice, trench feet & drying rooms also provision of waterproof bags for men for trenches. To ... brought back Sergt. Humphries. Clearing up correspondence, diary, censoring letters &c. Weather fine	E.F.M.

2353 Wt. W2544/1454 700,000 5/15 D. D. & L. A.D.S.S./Forms/C. 2118.

Army Form C. 2118.

WAR DIARY
or
~~INTELLIGENCE SUMMARY~~.

(*Erase heading not required.*)

Instructions regarding War Diaries and Intelligence Summaries are contained in F. S. Regs., Part II. and the Staff Manual respectively. Title pages will be prepared in manuscript.

Place	Date	Hour	Summary of Events and Information	Remarks and references to Appendices
	24/11/16		Capt. Messent, OC Sanitary Section 23rd Division, proceeded to England on leave: Capt. H.R. Macintyre, 69th Field Ambulance, assumed temporarily duties of OC Sanitary Section.	HKM
			Interviewed OC Sanitary Section 41st Division regarding use of Clayton Disinfector	
	25/11/16		Visited Laundry: arranged with OC Laundry regarding use of steam chamber for connection with Clayton Disinfector. Inspected Infantry Barracks, YPRES, with special reference to Food Storage: Selected site for storage of meat.	HKM
			Visited 8th Yorks Transport Lines, & advised regarding Cookhouse, Latrines, & Incinerator etc	
			Visited 23rd Divisional School & advised regarding incinerator, Cookhouse, & Latrines	
			Visited ADMS.	
	26/11/16		Visited YPRES:- Infantry Barracks re food Storage, & burying of excreta.	
			Inspected water tanks in YPRES, & sources of Supply from the MOAT: banks of moat fouled with excreta. Inspected Brigade HQ at RAMPARTS. Correspondence with ADMS regarding water supply from the MOAT at YPRES, & regarding removal of refuse from YPRES. Visited billets at the CLOISTERS, YPRES: inspected new latrine there.	HKM

Army Form C. 2118.

Instructions regarding War Diaries and Intelligence Summaries are contained in F. S. Regs., Part II. and the Staff Manual respectively. Title pages will be prepared in manuscript.

WAR DIARY

~~or~~

~~INTELLIGENCE SUMMARY.~~

(Erase heading not required.)

Place	Date	Hour	Summary of Events and Information	Remarks and references to Appendices
	27/11/16.		Visited R.E. Dump, ~~to~~ see constructional works in hand there by Sanitary Section. Inspected 10 West Ridings Transport lines, + transport lines of 70th Machine Gun Coy, + 8th Yorks + Lancs, + suggested improvements.	HKM
	28/11/16.		Visited Transport lines of 9th Yorks + of 9th Yorks + Lancs. + suggested improvements. Visited MONTREAL CAMP with special reference to arrangements for ablution + for disposal of excreta. Visited R.E. Dump with reference to construction of ~~door~~ for chamber for Clayton disinfector.	HKM
	29/11/16.		Visited with ADMS, the INFANTRY BARRACKS, HOSPICE, CLOISTERS, CAVALRY BARRACKS, + Brigade HQrs at YPRES, with special reference to food storage + ablution arrangements. Visited Divisional Laundry with view to fitting up Clayton disinfector which had been brought there. Clayton disinfector recalled by or Sanitary Section the same evening to 41st Div HQ on authority of DDMS X Corps.	HKM
	30/11/16.		Visited YPRES with reference to discovering source of water supply for ablution benches for HOSPICE + CLOISTERS. Site at the "SEWER" near CLOISTERS not considered satisfactory as being too open + exposed to shell fire. No wells found in convenient situation. Attended meeting of 23rd Div Medical Society in afternoon — lecture by Capt Stokes, RAMC. OC. No.1 Mobile Laboratory, on "Infective Jaundice".	HKM

2353 Wt. W2544/1454 700,000 5/15 D. D. & L. A.D.S.S./Forms/C. 2118.

Dec 1916

23rd Div

140/90.

Vol 16

Confidential

War Diary of O.C. 40th Sanitary Section, R.A.M.C.(T)
from December 1st to December 31st 1916.

(Volume 16).

Army Form C. 2118.

Instructions regarding War Diaries and Intelligence Summaries are contained in F. S. Regs., Part II. and the Staff Manual respectively. Title pages will be prepared in manuscript.

WAR DIARY
~~or~~
~~INTELLIGENCE SUMMARY.~~
(Erase heading not required.)

Place	Date	Hour	Summary of Events and Information	Remarks and references to Appendices
	1/12/16		Visited Regimental Aid Posts + some of trenches: interviewed the regimental medical officers of three of the battalions in the line regarding sanitary matters, disposal of dry refuse, water supplies, + trench latrines. Inspected the sanitary arrangements at the BUND with M.O. i/c 9th Yorks + Lancs advised. Inspected transport lines of 11th West Yorks, + advised on sanitary matters.	
	2/12/16		Visited R.E. dump re construction of shelter for ablution bench, YPRES, etc. Visited Infantry Barracks, YPRES, regarding storage of food, + re ablution benches + latrines. Visited CAVALRY BARRACKS, + the HOSPICE, YPRES, with M.O. i/c 8th KOYLI, re food storage + ablution arrangements. Inspected water tanks at RAMPARTS.	
	3/12/16		Inspected ST LAWRENCE + ERIE camps, + 70th Brigade HQ Transport. Inspected YMCA hut at ERIE camp: advised re disinfection of cups, + disposal of refuse. Clayton disinfecting machine fixed in position at 23rd Divisional laundry + tested.	
	4/12/16		Visited 23rd Divisional Laundry re Clayton disinfecting apparatus. Inspected water supplies at the MOAT, YPRES, at the SWIMMING BATH, (I.8.b.0.6. Sheet 28.) + at I.8.d.1.8., + also the two service tanks in use by 23rd Division at the RAMPARTS.	

2353 Wt. W2544/1454 700,000 5/15 D. D. & L. A.D.S.S./Forms/C. 2118.

Army Form C. 2118.

Instructions regarding War Diaries and Intelligence Summaries are contained in F. S. Regs., Part II. and the Staff Manual respectively. Title pages will be prepared in manuscript.

WAR DIARY

~~or~~

~~INTELLIGENCE SUMMARY.~~

(*Erase heading not required.*)

Place	Date	Hour	Summary of Events and Information	Remarks and references to Appendices
	5/12/16		Visited Infantry Barracks, YPRES, re ablution arrangements	HRm.
	6/12/16		Visited R.E. Dump re constructional work by Sanitary Section. Visited 23rd Divisional School & interviewed adjutant regarding Construction of Cookhouse & incinerator. Visited Staff Sergt Burnley at VLAMERTINGHE re work in his areas. Visited Div'l Laundry with reference to Clayton Disinfector	HRm.
	7.12.16		Returned from leave arriving billet about 10.15 a.m. Picking up threads re work from Capt MacIntyre. Visited Divl School & Baths with him. In afternoon to medical conference which owing to indisposition of ADMS was postponed. At D.R.S. with MacIntyre discussing re work. Correspondence &c. Weather Foggy.	EJM
	8.12.16		To Headqrs to see ADMS but he was out. Saw DADMS. Office work &c. In afternoon to YPRES inspected latrines at RAMPARTS & also ablution benches with Sergt ~~Chapman~~ Humphries. Brought him back to go on leave next day. On way to YPRES called at RE dump saw Cpl Cole. At ASYLUM made arrangements re billeting ~~constructional~~ party. In evening to see ADMS but he had gone to conference with General. Weather – To rain	EJM

2353 Wt W2544/1454 700,000 5/15 D. D. & L. A.D.S.S./Forms/C. 2118.

Instructions regarding War Diaries and Intelligence Summaries are contained in F. S. Regs., Part II. and the Staff Manual respectively. Title pages will be prepared in manuscript.

WAR DIARY
or
~~INTELLIGENCE~~ SUMMARY.

(Erase heading not required.)

Army Form C. 2118.

Place	Date	Hour	Summary of Events and Information	Remarks and references to Appendices
	9.12.16		To inspect camps of 23rd Div School & 69th Bde School & Toronto. Also transport lines of 8th Y. & L. Visited 70th Bde Canteen at Toronto Camp. See letter book for reports. Met Cpl Tabor at Toronto Camp. In afternoon drawing up reports, sketches &c. Diary, censoring letters. To see ADMS & spoke re chlorination treatment of laundry waste water, drying shed, water supply at YPRES & other minor matters & received instructions re same. Excused out door duty for a day or two owing to impetigo on face. Weather, fine	EJH
	10.12.16		Clearing up office papers, letters censoring, correspondence. To 91st F. Amb re face. Saw O.C. re Ford Car & Capt Picken. Reading notes &c re infective jaundice, & pamphlet on the louse problem. Day fairly well occupied with above matters, diary &c. Weather, to rain	EJH
	11.12.16		To Baths & inspected waste water treatment tanks, also drying rooms &c. Office work. On horse to inspect German prisoners camp re complaint of O.C. 191 Co ASC. To RE yard & saw Cpl Cole re work. Twelve traps for Infantry Barracks to be ready in 2 days. Reports, notes, diary &c. At 10.30 pm received DRLS letter from 23rd Div School & 11 ... telegram from ADMS to carry out disinfection of officers billets. Weather, to rain	EJH

2353 Wt. W2544/1454 700,000 5/15 D. D. & L. A.D.S.S./Forms/C. 2118.

Army Form C. 2118.

Instructions regarding War Diaries and Intelligence Summaries are contained in F. S. Regs., Part II. and the Staff Manual respectively. Title pages will be prepared in manuscript.

WAR DIARY
or
~~INTELLIGENCE SUMMARY.~~
(Erase heading not required.)

Place	Date	Hour	Summary of Events and Information	Remarks and references to Appendices
	12.12.16		To see O.C. 41st F. Amb. re car. To F. Cashier at MONTREAL CAMP on foot but arrived too late. Inspected camps of 9th Yorks Transport & MONTREAL CAMP (K.O.Y.L.I. saw Capt [illegible]). Visited [illegible] between these two camps (MONTREAL & WINNIPEG) & also the cinema canteen. Owing to no car went on foot. Read out sections of Army Regulations [illegible] (sections 4.5.6, 9 & 12) & also letter re German methods to obtain information from correspondence, to Section. Writing reports, letters &c. Weather Rain to snow to rain	EJM
	13.12.16		Office work. To inspect St LAWRENCE CAMP & also YMCA hut adjacent. Went on foot, no car. In afternoon in car [illegible] 8th Yks TRANSPORT & Ammn Dump near. On to YPRES [illegible] [illegible] [illegible] for INFANTRY BARRACKS. Saw Capt [illegible] HQ 11th W. Yks. Reports, notes, censoring letters, correspondence &c. Weather fine	EJM
	14.12.16		To YPRES to 128th Co. R.E. [illegible] Sergt Maj. to [illegible] BUND re water pipe repair. Inspected lake water supply, also latrines &c. Saw Capt [illegible] (13th N.F.) & M.O. 69th A.D.S. who accompanied me to ZILLEBEKE to see M.O. 11th N.F. re Infective Jaundice case. Enemy shelling ZILLEBEKE. To medical conference. Capt [illegible] gave paper on [illegible] in the trenches. Censoring letters, reports, correspondence. Weather fine to rain	EJM

2353 Wt. W2544/1454 700,000 5/15 D. D. & L. A.D.S.S./Forms/C. 2118.

Instructions regarding War Diaries and Intelligence Summaries are contained in F. S. Regs., Part II. and the Staff Manual respectively. Title pages will be prepared in manuscript.

WAR DIARY
or
~~INTELLIGENCE SUMMARY.~~

(Erase heading not required.)

Army Form C. 2118.

Place	Date	Hour	Summary of Events and Information	Remarks and references to Appendices
	15.12.16		To Divl Headqrs & inspected disinfection of Col Randolph's room. Saw ADMS who spoke re drying room with incinerator as heating agent. To 7 Ambce at ABEELE. Inspected water carts in afternoon with Cpl Bennet. Also Transport lines 11th W. Yks. Met A.P.M. Paid men, letters, report on plan of latrines submitted by R.E. correspondence. Weather fine	[illegible]
	16.12.16		To St LAWRENCE CAMP & saw C.O. & M.O. 11th W. Ridings re constructional work. On to YPRES & inspected dug outs Q.r Staff, 1st Aust. Tun. Co & 2nd Canadian Tun Co re RADMS sanitation report. Lunch with Q.r S. Staff. With M.O. inspected their billets, baths &c. Admirable arrangements & interest shown. Inspected Infantry barracks. Saw Capt. Drewin. Saw Capt Brunwell at the HOSPICE. Inspected the CLOISTERS with Capt Tribe also works at ablution shelter & A Tolkingham came in. Reports, answering letters, correspondence &c. Weather fine	[illegible]
	17.12.16		Received telegram to meet ADMS at RE dump re meat safe. Proceeded there via Divl Headqrs. Inspected incinerator near VLAMERTINGHE station. When at RE dump Col Hill spoke re sulphur disinfection of bedding re Col. Randolph. In afternoon to baths with Sgt Elkington. To forward area via [illegible] at VLA...E mill. With Col Fowler from BUND to HALFWAY HOUSE. Met MO (Winning) 84th & inspected latrines &c. Very satisfactory, oil drums with lid being used. Too dark to proceed further. Returned to billet 7.45 pm. Correspondence, diary &c. Weather fine	[illegible]

Instructions regarding War Diaries and Intelligence Summaries are contained in F. S. Regs., Part II. and the Staff Manual respectively. Title pages will be prepared in manuscript.

WAR DIARY
or
~~INTELLIGENCE SUMMARY.~~
(Erase heading not required.)

Army Form C. 2118.

Place	Date	Hour	Summary of Events and Information	Remarks and references to Appendices
	18.12.16		To see O.C. 71st Field Amb re [illegible]. To YPRES with Sanitary Officer YPRES inspected for sites of incinerators for the Inf. [illegible] Cavalry barracks, the ramparts & the hospice. Capt Tubb accompanied. In afternoon inspected camps of 70th M.G.C. & 154 R.G.C. Heavy Art. also progress of work at St LAWRENCE camp. Correspondence, answering, office work &c. Weather fine, cold.	[illegible]
	19.12.16		To WINNIPEG CAMP inspected same with Capt Berry 10th W Riding. To R.E. dump to inspect work being done. To [illegible] near VLAMERTINGHE ~~station~~ re ADMS letter. To V. mill to see Staff Sgt. In afternoon Capt Jones called re TORONTO CAMP. To 68th + 66th M.G.C. Transport lines where [illegible] the H Inf. These units about to move. To RE camp which was very satisfactory. Blizzard came on. Office work, diary, answering letters, correspondence & Weather. Snow storms.	[illegible]
	20.12.16		To Divisional Headqrs to see CRE re latrine shelter plan. To see ADMS but he was out. In afternoon to YPRES saw Town Major re incinerators also inspected [illegible] at [illegible] at [illegible] Barracks. Town being shelled. On return called at Div Headqrs. Had tea with Col [illegible] at C mess. Spoke ADMS re result of conversation with CRE this morning, he spoke re reinforcement camps, monthly sanitary work, told DADOS re latrine [illegible] and canvas waterproof bags. Correspondence, answering &c. Weather fine, cold.	[illegible]

2353 Wt. W2544/1454 700,000 5/15 D. D. & L. A.D.S.S./Forms/C. 2118.

Instructions regarding War Diaries and Intelligence Summaries are contained in F. S. Regs., Part II. and the Staff Manual respectively. Title pages will be prepared in manuscript.

WAR DIARY
or
~~INTELLIGENCE SUMMARY.~~
(Erase heading not required.)

Army Form C. 2118.

Place	Date	Hour	Summary of Events and Information	Remarks and references to Appendices
	21.12.16		Inspecting the three Brigade reinforcement camps. Drawing up plans & report on same. Saw CRE this morning & saw amended plan re latrines. To field cashier at RENINGHELST. Office work, diary, censoring &c. till after 11 pm. Weather, very wet [illegible]	EJM
	22.12.16		Sent reinforcement camp reports to [illegible] office. To meet Belgian gendarme to [illegible] [illegible] of [illegible] at [illegible] [illegible] on the OUDERDOM - VLAMERTINGHE ROAD. At RE dump saw Capt [illegible] who said no more material at present available. Took [illegible] to WINNIPEG CAMP but Capt BERRY had gone on leave. At SALVAGE Co DUMP for latrine pails but none available. In afternoon did not feel well but walked to [illegible] with Capt [illegible] & on the way inspected ordnance dump. Left message at Bath that I was sending man to CLAYTON DISINFECTOR tomorrow. Saw RAMC's report re waterproof bags for trenches, also re latrine pails & sanitary condition of camp. Saw Corps Water Officer re water [illegible] [illegible], censoring &c. Not feeling well turned in early (Had temp 101.2). Weather, Fine	EJM
	23.12.16		Did not get up till 10 a.m. To 71st F Amb. but did not go out again. Clearing up pile of papers to be filed &c. Censoring letters. Took matters easily today. Weather, Very strong gale	EJM

2353 Wt. W2544/1454 700,000 5/15 D. D. & L. A.D.S.S./Forms/C. 2118.

Instructions regarding War Diaries and Intelligence Summaries are contained in F. S. Regs., Part II. and the Staff Manual respectively. Title pages will be prepared in manuscript.

WAR DIARY
or
~~INTELLIGENCE SUMMARY.~~
(Erase heading not required.)

Army Form C. 2118.

Place	Date	Hour	Summary of Events and Information	Remarks and references to Appendices
	24.12.16		To visit camps of Brigade [illegible] at St Lawrence, Toronto & [illegible] road. The 40 Bde at TORONTO CAMP were making excellent progress but the other camps were very backward in [illegible] work. In afternoon to see ADMS but he was out, saw Capt [illegible] [illegible] re "[illegible] up [illegible]" &c. Office work correspondence, [illegible] &c. Few preparations for Xmas. Weather Very fine.	EJM
	25.12.16		Xmas. Practically no work. Men cleaned up camp &c. Dinner at 3.0 pm. ADMS came just after dinner to [illegible] a few words of thanks [illegible] to the men. To dinner in evening with 71st F. Ambulance. Weather, Windy, showers.	EJM
	26.12.16		Reorganising work & clearing up matters which came in over Xmas. To Div[l] Adj[t] [illegible] C.RE re [illegible] &c for BUND Scheme, he agreed to men working at yard & promised all material he could spare. In afternoon to [illegible] F Amb. at the Mill [illegible] [illegible] re arranging for working party at the BUND. Inspected camp of 19th M.G.C. At RE yard, instructions to Capt Cole re construction for BUND Scheme. Office work &c. Weather Very fine	EJM

2353 Wt. W2544/1454 700,000 5/15 D. D. & L. A.D.S.S./Forms/C. 2118.

Instructions regarding War Diaries and Intelligence Summaries are contained in F. S. Regs., Part II. and the Staff Manual respectively. Title pages will be prepared in manuscript.

WAR DIARY

or

~~INTELLIGENCE SUMMARY.~~

(Erase heading not required.)

Army Form C. 2118.

Place	Date	Hour	Summary of Events and Information	Remarks and references to Appendices
	27.12.16		Inspected camps of Salvage Co. 4/2 + 4/3 D.L.I. Transport during the morning. In afternoon inspected camps of 191 - 192 + 193 Coys A.S.C. These were generally satisfactory. Reports, diary, censoring letters &c. Weather fine.	EJM
	28.12.16		To R.E. Dump to see progress of work for Bu[illegible] scheme. Inspected 10th W. Riding Transport lines & T.M.B. (Heavy) camp. Also 98th Bde Reinforcement camp. Saw O.C. of camp but he was called away. Called at Divl H.Q. to see Adjutant R.E. In afternoon inspected water barrels, water clear at No 10, fairly so No 11 + 32 but at No 446 water not a good colour. Received call to go to see A.D.M.S. Called at Dg. & Q. re Bu[illegible] being sent up to-morrow. To see A.D.M.S. who instructed me to go to STEENVORDE re ~~Concentration~~ Camp. On with sanitary work report. Diary, correspondence notes &c. Weather fine, frosty.	EJM
	29.12.16		To STEENVORDE & met O.C. (Col. [illegible]) Inspected sites for sanitary constructions for concentration camp. Work appeared to be arranged for. Stayed to lunch with 90th F. Amb. On return inspected drying room with incinerator at Xth Corps Headqrs. Correspondence, censoring letters, reports &c. Weather / Windy, dull.	EJM.

2353 Wt. W2544/1454 700,000 5/15 D. D. & L. A.D.S.S./Forms/C. 2118.

Army Form C. 2118.

Instructions regarding War Diaries and Intelligence Summaries are contained in F. S. Regs., Part II. and the Staff Manual respectively. Title pages will be prepared in manuscript.

WAR DIARY

or

~~INTELLIGENCE SUMMARY.~~

(Erase heading not required.)

Place	Date	Hour	Summary of Events and Information	Remarks and references to Appendices
	30.12.16		Ford car ordered for 9.30am in order to proceed to YPRES. Owing to breakdown did not arrive till 12 noon. With Sgt Elkington to St LAWRENCE CAMP. One incinerator completed, second one started. Ablution shelter in hand but most of the material had been stolen for fire wood. Difficulties to carry out work seem almost insuperable. In afternoon to YPRES. Certain amount of shelling, particularly with aircraft guns. At Infantry Barracks saw MO (Capt Fisher) who requested another officers latrine be constructed. Inspected barracks. To RAMPARTS saw Sgt Humphreys re incinerators, work not started, difficulties about labour as Town Major was on leave. Saw Staff Capt. 70th Inf. Bde re incinerator to heat room at BARRACKS & Staff Capt. 69th Bde re a working party for incinerators. No satisfaction obtained in regard to the latter. Pointed out site for incinerator to Sgt Humphreys for the HOSPICE. He will get work under way. Usual office work. Weather, Mild & fine.	EJH
	31-12-16		To inspect camps for sanitary needs. Cpl Lewis accompanied me. Morning to 8th Yorks, 154th Bt. RGA. 70th M.G.C. Transport & Div camp. Saw OC 70th M.G.C. re cookhouse & OC Bomb School re removal of ablution fixtures. Afternoon at Toronto Camp (Bde School, Bath Camp, Reinforcement camp) & also 68th + 69th M.G.C. camps in course of construction. In morning called at Divl Head Qrs but ADMS & Capt Bell were out. Diary, notes &c. Weather, Dull.	EJH

2353 Wt. W2544/1454 700,000 5/15 D. D. & L. A.D.S.S./Forms/C. 2118.

Vol 17

CONFIDENTIAL.

War Diary of O.C. 40th Sanitary Section R.A.M.C. (T.F.)

(Volume 17).

(January 1st 1917 to January 31st 1917).

Army Form C. 2118.

WAR DIARY
or
~~INTELLIGENCE SUMMARY.~~
(Erase heading not required.)

Instructions regarding War Diaries and Intelligence Summaries are contained in F. S. Regs., Part II. and the Staff Manual respectively. Title pages will be prepared in manuscript.

Place	Date	Hour	Summary of Events and Information	Remarks and references to Appendices
YPRES (SECTOR)	1-1-17		On with sanitary summaries of camps. Inspected in the morning 1st Aust Tun. Co. 128th R.G.A. 4th to 8th Y. & L. Transport lines. To RE dump to see progress. To Div Head Qrs. ADMS was out. Saw C.R.E. re material for drying shed. In afternoon visited wagon lines D.102 Bde RFA & also transport lines 13th & 12th DLI & 10th N.F. In evening to see ADMS. Showed method of keeping camp sanitary records. Office work. Weather fine	EfM
	2.1.17		Preparation of sanitary summaries. Reports &c. In afternoon to inspect Notts & Derby Transport lines also to try & find another camp available for sections. Diary notes &c. Capt Knight Corps Sanitary Officer came in re Xth Corps School of Sanitation. Weather dull	EfM
	3.1.17		To the Mill. Saw O.C. 70th F. Amb. re working party for the BUND. To YPRES & inspected building of incinerators Infantry Barracks. Saw Sergt Humphries & showed plans for RAMPARTS incinerators & also inspected place for RE incinerator. To the BUND. Saw Capt Tabor & Capt Marsden re work. Same progressing owing to difficulties & also enemy shelling. Saw Lt Dobson 69th F. Amb. To see ADMS in evening. He spoke on phone to Col Wilkinson re no material from the Bde. Correspondence, censoring &c &c. Weather dull	EfM

2353 Wt. W2544/1454 700,000 5/15 D. D. & L. A.D.S.S./Forms/C. 2118.

Instructions regarding War Diaries and Intelligence Summaries are contained in F. S. Regs., Part II. and the Staff Manual respectively. Title pages will be prepared in manuscript.

WAR DIARY
or
~~INTELLIGENCE SUMMARY.~~
(Erase heading not required.)

Army Form C. 2118.

Place	Date	Hour	Summary of Events and Information	Remarks and references to Appendices
	4.1.17		To DRS with OC 69th F Amb inspected camp. To field [illegible]. Capt Shaw RAMC came — went to RENINGHELST. To St LAWRENCE CAMP saw M.O. 9th Y&L re fitting [illegible] with 2nd in command. Also inspected reinforcement camp & suggested brick flooring to cook house. In afternoon to 70th Bde School re a lot [illegible] material for [illegible]. Apparently it was for 69th Bde School. ~~To RE dump.~~ At WINNIPEG CAMP to choose site for drying room with M.O. [illegible]. Office work reports &c. Weather fine.	[illegible]
	5.1.17		Inspecting work at camp. [illegible] from 69th reported for duty. To see Adjutant RE but he was out. To St LAWRENCE CAMP. Saw Cpl Penfold at work at ablution bench. Saw M.O. re [illegible] material. Saw officer i/c 69th Bde School re telegram. He promised to carry out all work. I mentioned re bringing latrines nearer huts. To RE Dump to make arrangements re materials. In afternoon inspected camp of 13th DLI Transport & B & C Bty Wagon Lines 103 Bde RFA. These camps are in a deplorable condition. Lieut Staff [illegible]. He returned to billet with me. Office work &c. Weather fine	[illegible]

2353 Wt. W2544/1454 700,000 5/15 D. D. & L. A.D.S.S./Forms/C. 2118.

Army Form C. 2118.

WAR DIARY
or
~~INTELLIGENCE SUMMARY~~
(Erase heading not required.)

Instructions regarding War Diaries and Intelligence Summaries are contained in F. S. Regs., Part II. and the Staff Manual respectively. Title pages will be prepared in manuscript.

Place	Date	Hour	Summary of Events and Information	Remarks and references to Appendices
	6.1.17		To see Zollie's Officer re Clayton Machine. This case & running. Inspected est'amenities POPERINGHE - WESTOUTRE ROAD. Inspected camp No 1 Section D.A.C. To see Colonel Buchanan D.A.C. In afternoon to R.E. dump. Met Capt Eddleston there & spoke re material. To Divl Headqrs & saw Col Gibson acting ADMS. In evening to cinema with Capt Pearson 69th F. Amb. & dinner at O. Club. Weather, Dull	[illegible]
	7.1.17		Clearing up clerical work, diary, notes, indexing &c. To inspect camp No 3 Section D.A.C. In afternoon inspecting frame work of drying room. To see O.C. 70th F. Amb. re a bricklayer but he was out. To inspect 68th Bde Reinforcement Camp. Little or no progress made — sanitary constructional work. To inspect ammn. dump D.A.C. Correspondence, reports &c. Weather, Dull to showery.	[illegible]
	8.1.17		To set out site for drying hut at WINNIPEG CAMP. Inspected 102nd Co. R.E. Camp. Saw Capt Dobb when leaving. In afternoon inspected camps of Divisional School (with Commandant) & wagon lines of 101st & 126th Cos. R.E. Writing reports, correspondence &c. Capt [illegible] returned from leave. Weather, Showery	[illegible]

2353 Wt. W2544/1454 700,000 5/15 D. D. & L. A.D.S.S./Forms/C. 2118.

Instructions regarding War Diaries and Intelligence Summaries are contained in F. S. Regs., Part II. and the Staff Manual respectively. Title pages will be prepared in manuscript.

WAR DIARY
or
~~INTELLIGENCE SUMMARY.~~
(Erase heading not required.)

Army Form C. 2118.

Place	Date	Hour	Summary of Events and Information	Remarks and references to Appendices
	9.1.17		To get works started at WINNIPEG CAMP on the drying shed. Saw O.C. & M.O. 10th W Riding & obtained two bricklayers. To R.E. Yard arranging re material. To C 102 Bde RFA camp. In afternoon to CRE re material & also ADMS office but no one in. To YPRES saw Sanitary Officer re water tank – (baths being cleaned). Owing to shelling not able to carry out any inspections. Weather, Showery	E.J.M.
	10.1.17		Preparing lectures & plans for Xth Corps School of Sanitation on Refuse destructors disposal &c. ~~Water~~ & Water Supplies &c. Very heavy bombardment proceeding all day. POPERINGHE was shelled in afternoon. Was sent to Baths Officer. Paid men. Correspondence, diary &c. Weather, Dull to fine	E.J.M.
	11.1.17		To Xth Corps School of Sanitation to lecture, morning & afternoon. Called at ADMS on return. Had tea at C Mess. Cpl Tabor returned. Reports, correspondence, censoring &c. Weather, Rain to snow	E.J.M.
	12.1.17		To see progress of work at drying shed. Via KRUISSTRAAT to YPRES. Inspected incinerators for Bde Headqrs (under construction) R.E. (under construction) INFANTRY BARRACKS, burning but large amount of refuse to dispose of. Saw M.O. (Haynes) N.F. re meat safe at I. BARRACKS. Inspection at I Barracks. Inspection of dug outs at RAMPART & at drying shed & RE yard re progress of work. At St LAWRENCE CAMP. Reports, correspondence &c. Weather, Dull, wet	E.J.M.

2353 Wt. W2544/1454 700,000 5/15 D. D. & L. A.D.S.S./Forms/C. 2118.

Army Form C. 2118.

WAR DIARY
or
~~INTELLIGENCE SUMMARY.~~
(Erase heading not required.)

Instructions regarding War Diaries and Intelligence Summaries are contained in F. S. Regs., Part II. and the Staff Manual respectively. Title pages will be prepared in manuscript.

Place	Date	Hour	Summary of Events and Information	Remarks and references to Appendices
	13.1.17		To WINNIPEG CAMP supervising erection of drying hut. Owing to exceedingly bad weather work delayed & camp inspection more or less impracticable. On with sanitary reports of camps, correspondence, censoring & [illegible] [illegible] forwarded on leave. Weather very bad, wet.	[illegible]
	14.1.17.		To meet Belgian [illegible] at [illegible] at VLAMERTINGHE. [illegible] On to YPRES & to the BUND inspecting work in progress. With Capt Dawkins to STAFFORD STREET, MAPLE COPSE &c. On return called to see O.C. 7th F. Amb re brick for BUND scheme. Office work, censoring &c. Weather fine, misty.	[illegible]
	15.1.17		To inspect work at drying shed & R.E. dump. To Div [illegible] re constructional work also saw C.R.E. re brick & [illegible] for [illegible]. In afternoon inspected camp of 190th Co A.S.C. & 8th Yorks Transport lines. Reports, correspondence, &c. Weather fine, misty	[illegible]
	16.1.17.		Inspected wagon lines C & A 102nd Bde R.F.A. with Capt Ridley, also work at drying shed. Drew 1000 francs at field cashier. [illegible] [illegible]. In afternoon inspected 9th Yorks Transport & 68th Bde Reinforcement Camp met Staff Sgt at latter. Correspondence, [illegible] &c. Weather fine, cold	[illegible]

2353 Wt. W2544/1454 700,000 5/15 D. D. & L. A.D.S.S./Forms/C. 2118.

Instructions regarding War Diaries and Intelligence Summaries are contained in F. S. Regs., Part II. and the Staff Manual respectively. Title pages will be prepared in manuscript.

WAR DIARY
or
~~INTELLIGENCE SUMMARY.~~
(Erase heading not required.)

Army Form C. 2118.

Place	Date	Hour	Summary of Events and Information	Remarks and references to Appendices
	17.1.17		To TORONTO & ST LAWRENCE CAMPS. Saw M.O. (Capt Doyle) re paratyphoid case. To 40th F. Amb. re the drill. At WINNIPEG CAMP saw M.O. (Capt Scott) re [illegible] for drying hut. Owing to continuous fall of snow did not go out in the afternoon. On with Sanitary reports, censoring, diary, correspondence &c. Weather Snow	E.J.M.
	18.1.17		To Xth Corp. School of Sanitation to give weekly lecture. Lunch with Capt Ross. Returned straight from BOESCHEPE to camp. Office work. Weather Snow.	E.J.M.
	19.1.17		Journey to give lecture Xth Corp Sanitation School. Inspected Transport lines of 9th S. Staffs & 8th K.O.Y.L.I. Saw L/Sneed. Inspected drying hut. In afternoon inspected wagon lines B Batty 102 Bde R.F.A. Writing reports on camps, censoring letters &c. Weather Dull	E.J.M.
	20.1.17		Inspected 68th M.G.C. camp also transport lines 9th Yorks & Divl. Canteen + MONTREAL CAMP. In afternoon inspected D Batt 102 Bde RFA wagon lines. To see Salvage Officer. To see acting ADMS. Had tea with "C" Mess. Office work &c. Weather, Dull	E.J.M.

2353 Wt W2544/1454 700,000 5/15 D. D. & L. A.D.S.S./Forms/C. 2118.

Army Form C. 2118.

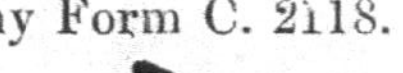

WAR DIARY
or
~~INTELLIGENCE SUMMARY.~~
(Erase heading not required.)

Instructions regarding War Diaries and Intelligence Summaries are contained in F. S. Regs., Part II. and the Staff Manual respectively. Title pages will be prepared in manuscript.

Place	Date	Hour	Summary of Events and Information	Remarks and references to Appendices
	21.1.17		To Div. School Camp saw 2nd in Command re latrines. To Baltic Pop. saw Capt MORAN re temporary incinerator. Inspected No 2 Section D.A.C. camp. Supervised work in progress at camp. Reports, correspondence, censoring letters &c. Weather, dull, frosty	EJM
	22.1.17		To see drying shed. To INFANTRY BARRACKS YPRES. Saw Capt Blake & Riddle. In afternoon to see re infection case 70th Bde School, also inspected camp. To TORONTO CAMP & REINFORCEMENT CAMP inspected same with Capt ROWER 11th R.F. In evening to see ADMS would an hour & half but he did not come. Reports, diary &c. Weather, fine cold	EJM
	23.1.17		Ford ambulance broke down so went on foot to see work at shed baths at R.E. Yard. In afternoon inspected A.B. & D Bty 103rd Bde R.F.A. with Staff Sgt. In evening to see ADMS also saw Col Wilkinson re another bath. Censoring &c. Weather, fine, cold	EJM
	24.1.17		Writing reports &c. To VLAMERTINGHE Mill. Met ADMS there. To see bath. In afternoon inspected M.V.S. camp. Then ADMS said he was to inspect "mange isolation camp". Bland office work. Weather, fine, cold	EJM

2353 Wt. W2544/1454 700,000 5/15 D. D. & L. A.D.S.S./Forms/C. 2118.

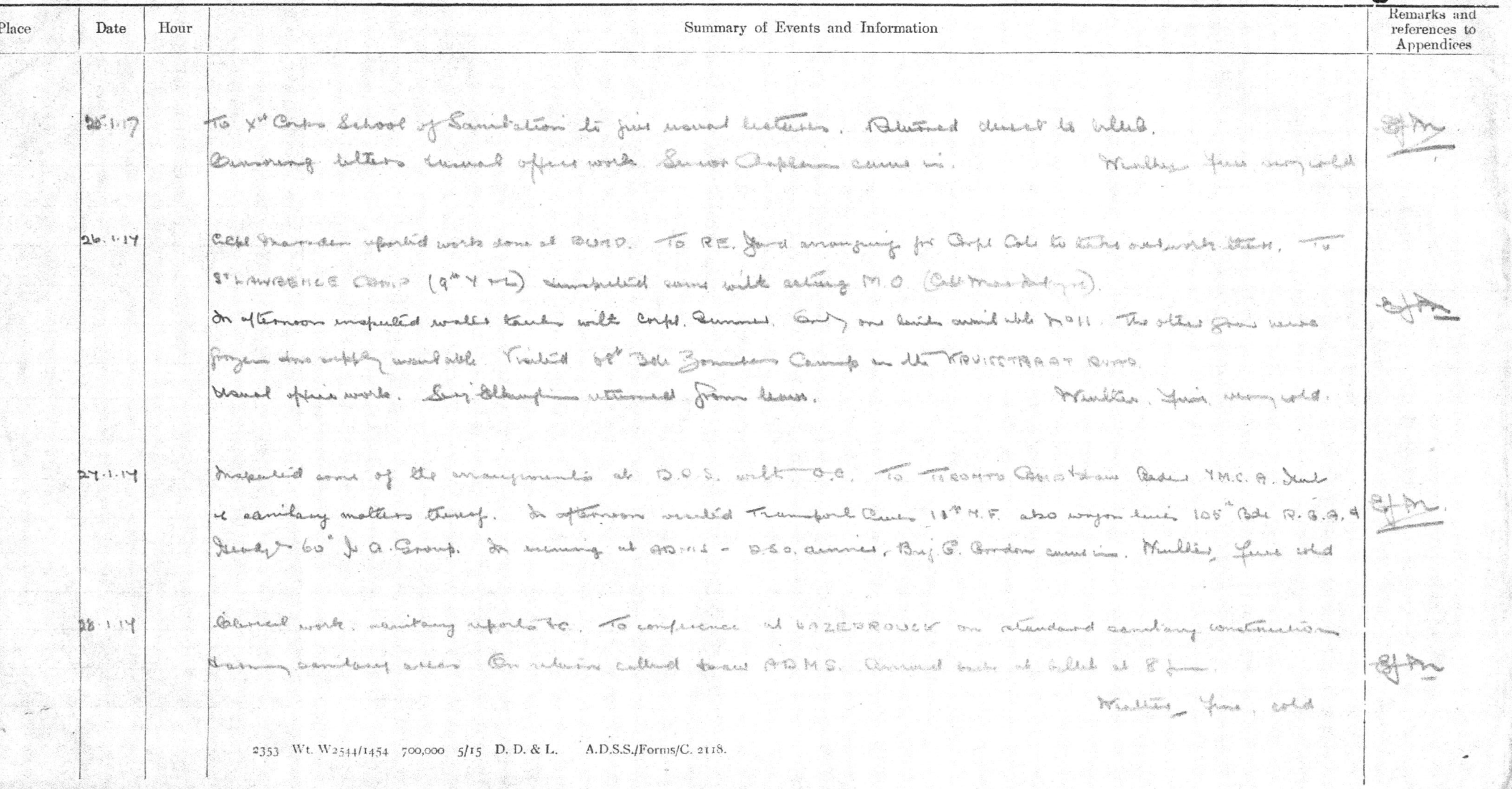

Instructions regarding War Diaries and Intelligence Summaries are contained in F. S. Regs., Part II. and the Staff Manual respectively. Title pages will be prepared in manuscript.

WAR DIARY
or
~~INTELLIGENCE SUMMARY.~~
(Erase heading not required.)

Army Form C. 2118.

Place	Date	Hour	Summary of Events and Information	Remarks and references to Appendices
	25.1.17		To Xth Corps School of Sanitation to give usual lecture. Returned direct to billet. Censoring letters usual office work. Senior Chaplain came in. Weather fine very cold	[illegible]
	26.1.17		[illegible] reported works done at BURD. To R.E. Yard arranging for Corpl Cole to take out [illegible]. To St LAWRENCE CAMP (9th Y [illegible]) inspected same with acting M.O. ([illegible]). In afternoon inspected water tanks with Corpl. [illegible]. Only one [illegible] No 11. The other [illegible] were frozen [illegible] supply [illegible]. Visited [illegible] Bde [illegible] Camp on the KRUISSTRAAT ROAD. Usual office work. [illegible] returned from leave. Weather fair, very cold.	[illegible]
	27.1.17		Inspected some of the arrangements at D.O.S. with O.C. To [illegible] YMCA [illegible] re sanitary matters thereof. In afternoon visited Transport Lines 11th [illegible] also wagon lines 105th Bde R.G.A. & [illegible] 60th [illegible] Group. In evening at ADMS – D.S.O. [illegible], Brig. G. Gordon came in. Weather fine cold	[illegible]
	28.1.17		Clerical work, sanitary reports &c. To conference at HAZEBROUCK on standard sanitary construction [illegible] sanitary areas. On return called to see A.D.M.S. Arrived back at billet at 8 pm. Weather fine, cold	[illegible]

2353 Wt. W2544/1454 700,000 5/15 D. D. & L. A.D.S.S./Forms/C. 2118.

Instructions regarding War Diaries and Intelligence Summaries are contained in F. S. Regs., Part II. and the Staff Manual respectively. Title pages will be prepared in manuscript.

WAR DIARY
or
~~INTELLIGENCE SUMMARY.~~
(Erase heading not required.)

Army Form C. 2118.

Place	Date	Hour	Summary of Events and Information	Remarks and references to Appendices
	29.1.17		On foot inspected 47th Div. [illegible] Camp also B 102 Wagon lines & 11th W. Yorks Transport Lines. In afternoon to see Capt MacIntyre re formation of Divl Health Section. Inspected [illegible] Camp & also YMCA hut. Saw O.C. 7th T.M.B. re latrines. Usual office work. Weather, very cold.	[illegible]
	30.1.17		To YPRES to meet Sanitary Officer but he did not turn up. Inspected [illegible] Barracks with [illegible]. To Cavalry Barracks to meet Capt Mackenzie inspected his sanitary apparatus &c. In afternoon on horseback to see Capt MacIntyre then CRE [illegible] & called at Salvage Officer re old [illegible]. Reports correspondence &c. Weather, occasional snow cold.	[illegible]
	31.1.17		Office work. Circulars to O.C. men on [illegible] duties. To HAZEBROUCK to conference re [illegible] of scheme for destruction of rats. On return called at ADMS saw ADMS office waiting for a while. Nothing of importance to note. Arrived back 8.15 pm. Weather, occasional snow, cold.	[illegible]

2353 Wt. W2544/1454 700,000 5/15 D. D. & L. A.D.S.S./Forms/C. 2118.

23/9/Tx1

Feb. 1917

Confidential

140/991 Vol 18

War Diary of

O.C. 40th Sanitary Section R.A.M.C. (T)

(February 1st to February 28th 1917.)

(Volume. 18).

Army Form C. 2118.

Instructions regarding War Diaries and Intelligence Summaries are contained in F. S. Regs., Part II. and the Staff Manual respectively. Title pages will be prepared in manuscript.

WAR DIARY
or
~~INTELLIGENCE SUMMARY.~~
(Erase heading not required.)

Place	Date	Hour	Summary of Events and Information	Remarks and references to Appendices
NEAR POPERINGHE	1.2.17		To give lectures at X Corps School of Sanitation. Clearing up reports, office work &c. Censoring letters. Weather, fine, cold	E.J.M.
	2.2.17		With Capt. MacIntyre to 70th F. Amb. VLAMERTINGHE & spoke re sending one more personnel & also re material for ... of R.E. Yard & also inspected drying shed. Saw ADMS at 70th F. Amb. & we spoke re "Health Section" programme. In afternoon inspected transport lines of 8th Yorks & 10th N.F. & also found of 12th DLI. Office work, correspondence &c. Weather, fine, cold	E.J.M.
	3.2.17		On foot inspected Prisoners of War Camp with Capt. Llewellyn & also transport lines 12th DLI & wagon lines D.102. In afternoon inspected wagon lines 103rd Bde R.F.A. Had tea with wagon line officers. Office work, correspondence &c. Weather, fine, cold	E.J.M.
	4.2.17		On horse to RENINGHELST & saw C.R.E. (who was leaving division (Col Brunner)). Spoke re materials to Adjutant & to R.E. Yard to see progress of work. In afternoon on with Sanitary files. Called at ADMS office in morning but ADMS was out. Weather fine cold	E.J.M.

2353 Wt. W2544/1454 700,000 5/15 D. D. & L. A.D.S.S./Forms/C. 2118.

Instructions regarding War Diaries and Intelligence Summaries are contained in F. S. Regs., Part II. and the Staff Manual respectively. Title pages will be prepared in manuscript.

WAR DIARY
or
INTELLIGENCE SUMMARY.
(Erase heading not required.)

Army Form C. 2118.

Place	Date	Hour	Summary of Events and Information	Remarks and references to Appendices
	5.2.17		With Capt Macintyre interviewing men for health section. To YPRES with him inspected cookhouses at ramparts. Met ADMS at Inf Barracks re clean. Transport Officer making dry heat disinfector. To 70th F Amb at the Mill. Had lunch there. At YMCA and at TORONTO CAMP. Censoring letters, office work &. Weather fine cold	E.J.M.
	6.2.17		With Capt Macintyre to WINNIPEG. Met Capt Bean M.O. 10th W. Riding inspected incinerators & insanitary urinal. To R.E. dump arranged for grease traps to be made. At 10th M.F. Transport lines making enquiries re suspect enteric carrier. In afternoon clearing up correspondence. Writing office reports re inspection No 2 Section D.T.C. Weather fine cold	E.J.M.
	7.2.17		At 9 am to ADMS office. Saw ADMS also Belgian Interpreters re cantonment inspection, new system. Notes for ADMS re. In afternoon inspected camp 12th Div. 1. Transport lines called at 103rd Bde RFA & clearing up office work. Weather fine cold	E.J.M.
	8.2.17		To X Corps School of Sanitation to give usual lectures. Nothing else of import to note. Weather fine cold	E.J.M.
	9.2.17		Censoring letters, dispatching correspondence & interviewing men from ambulances for Health Detachment. Belgian Interpreters came with Capt Gunner commenced inspection of cantonment & Capt Calpin 41st Div San Sec came re inspection of respective areas. Arrangements for placing men of health detachment. Weather fine cold	E.J.M.

2353 Wt. W2544/1454 700,000 5/15 D. D. & L. A.D.S.S./Forms/C. 2118.

Instructions regarding War Diaries and Intelligence Summaries are contained in F. S. Regs., Part II. and the Staff Manual respectively. Title pages will be prepared in manuscript.

WAR DIARY
or
~~INTELLIGENCE SUMMARY.~~
(Erase heading not required.)

Army Form C. 2118.

Place	Date	Hour	Summary of Events and Information	Remarks and references to Appendices
	10.2.16		At 9 a.m. to Mange Horse Segregation Camp re burial of 8 horses. Owing to frost R.E. were there to blast the ground for trench to bury the horses. To inspect 8" How. Batt. Motor Transport temporary camp. To Reinforcement Camp 69th Bde re material required to complete camp, also inspected YMCA hut very unsatisfactory. Inspected ERIE camp. Owing to no car being available & horse being sick not able to proceed to inspect other reinforcement camps this afternoon. Office work reports diary &c. Weather fine, cold	E.J.M.
	11.2.16		To YPRES via car 69th F Amb to Mill [illegible] by [illegible] F Amb car. At [illegible] Barrack to meet 8 Officers + [illegible] YPRES but he did not arrive. Inspected the BARRACKS with Lt [illegible] M.O. 9th Y & L & Capt [illegible] To the PRISON saw S.C. who said he did not understand so was to meet me [illegible] matters. Returned to the [illegible] there. ADMS also there. He had inspected camp the morning. On return at reinforcement camps 69th & 70th Bdes. also YMCA hut TORONTO CAMP. Usual office work. Weather, fine, thaw commenced	E.J.M.
	12.2.16		Much clerical work various reports, arrangements &c. To drying shed where work has commenced. To ST LAWRENCE CAMP & inspected same with Lt [illegible] M.O. 10th N.F. Found camp had been left in a deplorable condition. Inspected a coffee house re complaint [illegible] In afternoon to [illegible] for money. Paid men. Drawing up reports &c. Weather fine, milder	E.J.M.
	13.2.16		Completing report on water [illegible]. To superintend work at drying shed & also inspect [illegible] In afternoon met Staff Sgt [illegible] & Sgt [illegible] inspected 68th Bde [illegible] School with Adjutant [illegible] to Mill & 70th F Amb) to [illegible]. Correspondence reports &c. Weather fine mild	E.J.M.

2353 Wt. W2544/1454 700,000 5/15 D. D. & L. A.D.S.S./Forms/C. 2118.

Army Form C. 2118.

Instructions regarding War Diaries and Intelligence Summaries are contained in F. S. Regs., Part II. and the Staff Manual respectively. Title pages will be prepared in manuscript.

WAR DIARY
or
~~INTELLIGENCE~~ SUMMARY.

(Erase heading not required.)

Place	Date	Hour	Summary of Events and Information	Remarks and references to Appendices
	14.2.17		Inspected work at drying shed & R.E. Yard. To 40th F. Amb. at their [illegible] re use of German [illegible]. To 60th H.A. Group to see M.O. re [illegible] but he was out. Phoned in afternoon [illegible] M.O. At Medical conference in afternoon. Reports, correspondence &c. Weather Fine, cold	[initials]
	15.2.17		To X Corps School of Sanitation to lecture morning & afternoon. Car late in calling for me at RENINGHELST. Usual office work. Weather Fine, cold	[initials]
	16.2.17		To inspect work at drying shed & R.E. Yard. To see M.O. 8th Yorks at KRUISSTRAAT re latrines. Visit 70th F. Amb. re mumps case Tunnelling C. A.I.F. To ST LAWRENCE CAMP to inspect incinerator construction. In afternoon attended lecture by CAPT ELLIS. RAMC. 10 C.C.S. at BAILLEUL on [illegible]. Called at ADMS office on return but he did not come in. On [illegible] to D.R.S. with [illegible] accident occurred thro' Belgian soldier riding his horse into the Ford Car. Weather, Dull, mild	[initials]
	17.2.17		To YPRES. Inspected billets 101st Co. R.E. also at INFANTRY BARRACKS. To BUND inspected latrines & other work. On our return called at R.E. Yard & gave instructions to Corpl Cole re work. Correspondence &c. In evening saw ADMS but nothing of importance to report. He spoke re complaint of 69 Bde [illegible] re water supply at YPRES. Weather, Dull mild	[initials]
	18.2.17		Dispatching 14 men of Health Section to X Corps School of Sanitation. Office work &c. Inspecting wagon lines C 102nd Bde & C 103rd Bde. Also called at drying shed & R.E. Yard. Kit inspection & billet inspection. Office work, reports &c. Weather, Dull mild	[initials]
	19.2.17		Inspected transport lines 11th W. Yorks & wagon lines A 102nd Bde RFA also ST LAWRENCE & ERIE CAMP. Saw Sergt Thompson at latter & found he had much improved conditions. Three incinerators in course of erection. In afternoon arranging re incinerators at WINNIPEG CAMP & saw M.O. 8th Y. & L. Also saw Cpl Cole. Answering letters on sanitary files &c. DADMS spoke on DRS phone re water test YPRES [illegible]. Carried out poisons test. Weather Dull, mild	[initials]

2353 Wt. W2514/1454 700,000 5/15 D. D. & L. A.D.S.S./Forms/C. 2118.

Instructions regarding War Diaries and Intelligence Summaries are contained in F. S. Regs., Part II. and the Staff Manual respectively. Title pages will be prepared in manuscript.

WAR DIARY
or
INTELLIGENCE SUMMARY.
(Erase heading not required.)

Army Form C. 2118.

Place	Date	Hour	Summary of Events and Information	Remarks and references to Appendices
	20.2.17		To see incinerator started at drying shed also to RE Dump. Returned early in view of any development in [illegible] at Most YPRES. On sanitary plan. Inspected camps Old Dump. M.V.C. & Sections 1 the D.A.C. Usual office work. [illegible] DADMS [illegible]. Weather, Dull, wet	[initials]
	21.2.17		Dealing with charge against [illegible] [illegible] absence of lights on lorry. To drying shed. [illegible] Cpl Gunner down to YPRES [illegible] BUND. In afternoon on [illegible] [illegible] with Cpl Gunner. To inspect D/102 Wagon Lines. Acting OC San. Sec. 39th Div. called during afternoon. Weather, Dull.	[initials]
	22.2.17		Waiting for O.C. San Sec. 39th Div. to come out he failed to put in an appearance. This prevented my inspection. In afternoon [illegible] to 'C' [illegible]. At ADMS Office [illegible] Capt [illegible] [illegible] [illegible]. [illegible] to make my own arrangement. To drying shed & RE Yard. 68th F. Amb. [illegible] to ADMS. Weather. Dull.	[initials]
	23.2.17		Lorry & party sent to EPERLECQUES. To X Corp. School of San. [illegible] [illegible] from [illegible]. Arrangement of [illegible]. Weather Dull	[initials]
	24.2.17		Going through office papers. Expected arrival of a party from relieving Section but none came. Inspection of camp [illegible]. Second party sent off. [illegible] Weather. Dull	[initials]
	25.2.17		To inspect various camps. Saw M.O.s of 11th Sussex & at WINNIPEG & MONTREAL CAMPS but they said they had not inspected the camps but had no complaints made. The former saying that the advance party said [illegible] was the cleanest camp they had taken over. At drying hut also saw T.O.s 9th Yorks, 10th W. Ridings & 8th [illegible] also a chaplain at 70th Bde School re sanitary [illegible]. In afternoon [illegible] over party 39 Div arrived. Sent urgent note [illegible] re relief. Spoke Capt [illegible] re [illegible] necessary [illegible] work could start at New D. H.Q. Weather, Dull	[initials]

2353 Wt. W2544/1454 700,000 5/15 D. D. & L. A.D.S.S./Forms/C. 2118.

Instructions regarding War Diaries and Intelligence Summaries are contained in F. S. Regs., Part II. and the Staff Manual respectively. Title pages will be prepared in manuscript.

WAR DIARY
or
~~INTELLIGENCE~~ SUMMARY

(Erase heading not required.)

Army Form C. 2118.

Place	Date	Hour	Summary of Events and Information	Remarks and references to Appendices
HOULLE	26.2.17		Spoke ADMS re delay probable in erecting sanitary constructions at D.H.Q. Set off in lorry remainder of section to new area at 10.30 am — At ABEELE saw Xth Corps Camp Commandant re (Lieut) Tabor & arranged to leave him till relief arrived. Saw Area Commandant at STEENVOORDE & he said I could take the lorry. Arrived HOULLE about 2 pm & lorry set off again immediately to be ready for ADMS material tomorrow. Weather fine.	[illegible]
	27.2.17		Detailing duties for men. On horse to DHQ St OMER & fixing up sanitary arrangements of which there were none. Saw San Officer S OMER (also Capt Key). Lorry returned late with material owing to being 'bogged' on road. ADMS spoke re matter of taking men from Xth Corps before relief arrived. The 39th Div San Sec had seemed to be very slack in the matter of taking over. After fixing up arrangements at D.H.Q. returned on lorry with [illegible] leaving a little after 8 pm. Weather dull.	[illegible]
	28.2.17		Detailing parties for inspecting areas. Correspondence, answering letters &c. Discussion with Staff Sergt re not reporting with guard for putting lorry. Walk with Capt Hawkes to find billet per orders. Met Staff Capt 69th Bde & walked round for billet but without success. He said I could keep present men's billet & would have officer's billet which I mentioned. In afternoon on bicycle to D.H.Q. to see if sanitary arrangements were satisfactory. Saw Capt [illegible] who said that matters could be left with him. Saw ADMS but he had nothing to discuss. Returned with Capt Brownell on Ford and car. Preparing Sanitary Standing Orders for Summer Campaigning, reports re withdrawal of personnel from Xth Corps &c &c. Party sent to 71st F Amb this morning for the MORDAUSQUES area. Weather dull.	[illegible]

Mar. 1917.

23rd Div.

140/2043 Vol 19

23

WAR : DIARY :

O.C. SANITARY : SECTION : 40

MARCH : 1917 :

Instructions regarding War Diaries and Intelligence Summaries are contained in F. S. Regs., Part II. and the Staff Manual respectively. Title pages will be prepared in manuscript.

WAR DIARY

or

~~INTELLIGENCE SUMMARY.~~

(Erase heading not required.)

Army Form C. 2118.

Place	Date	Hour	Summary of Events and Information	Remarks and references to Appendices
HOULLE	1-3-17		On with preparation of Sanitary Standing Orders for ~~Summer Campaigning~~. Drafting out forms for use in weekly sanitary report. Getting out sketches for water lectures. Had early lunch & proceeded on foot via EPERLECQUES to MORDAUSQUES. At E. met Capt Macintyre but ~~troops~~ not arrived also on to BAYEMHAM-LES-EPERLECQUES but only advance party of 69th M.G.C. arrived. At M. inspected various billets & wells also spring from which 71st F Amb. water supply is being drawn. Units inspected were 71st F Amb (part of) & 11th Notts & Derby (part of). Saw M.O. of latter & said water carts must be utilized also suggested narrow trench latrines in lieu of pits & wide latrines. Saw ~~O.C.~~ 71st F.A. & had tea, he said he would write me when he would like me to give water cart lecture. Returned in ambulance [illegible]. Ambulance from 70th F Amb had called for Sgt Chapman & party for YOLKERINCKHOVE with 71st F.A. Div. Weather fine. Usual clerical routine	EJM
	2.3.17		To inspect 8th Yorks at HOULLE with M.O. Met ADMS [illegible] [illegible] with him. Carried on with inspection of billets with M.O. Same fairly satisfactory. In afternoon with Capt DUNCAN on [illegible] to carry out reconnaissance for ADMS scheme. On with reports, standing orders &c. Car reported from 69th F Amb at mid day. Weather dull, cool.	EJM
	3.3.17		In Ford car to see O.C. 69th F Amb re lectures. With M.O. 10th W. Riding to inspect his battalion billets. Also saw M.O. 11th W. Yorks. In afternoon with Capt. DUNCAN, BERRY, & RIDDLE on reconnaissance for ADMS scheme. Working out scheme. Correspondence &c. O.C. Bricks came this morning but I was out. Weather dull, cool.	EJM
	4.3.17		To M.V.C. re my horse. Sergt of AVC came & said it was all right. To MOULLE & with M.O. 9th Yorks inspected billets of Bn. Same were fair but only wide trenches in use. In afternoon O.C. [illegible] Bde called re ambulance car. To meeting of ADMS at INGHEM re scheme. Spoke ADMS re Ford car re BROWNES. Censoring letters, correspondence &c. Weather fine, cool	EJM

2353 Wt. W2514/1454 700,000 5/15 D. D. & L. A.D.S.S./Forms/C. 2118.

Instructions regarding War Diaries and Intelligence Summaries are contained in F. S. Regs., Part II. and the Staff Manual respectively. Title pages will be prepared in manuscript.

WAR DIARY
or
~~INTELLIGENCE SUMMARY.~~
(Erase heading not required.)

Army Form C. 2118.

Place	Date	Hour	Summary of Events and Information	Remarks and references to Appendices
	5.3.17		Clearing up office work. To ARQUES inspected Divl Header party's billets. Met Camp Commandant there. On return called at Divl Laundry. Saw Capt. Macintyre, also at S^T OMER S.O. office but he was out. In afternoon inspected billets of 11th W. Yks at WESTROVE then to 103rd Bde R.F.A. Saw M.O. & advised precautions re diphtheria case. Arrived back at 7 p.m. Used Ford car in morning & horse in afternoon. Drawing up reports &c. Weather – Dull, cold.	[illegible]
	6.3.17		To 69th F. Amb to give lecture on water. Met ADMS who spoke re 103rd Bde RFA diphtheria case. In afternoon much correspondence to clear off also did not feel very grand. Weather fine, cold.	[illegible]
	7.3.17		To 71st F. Amb at MORDAUSQUES & gave water lecture. Lunched with Amb. In afternoon to TOURNEHEM & gave demonstration on travelling kitchens & water carts to 70th Inf Bde. Tea with Amb. Usual clerical work. Weather, Easterly wind very cold.	[illegible]
	8.3.17		Expected Ford car at 9.30 a.m. but it did not arrive till 11 a.m. To inspect 8th K.O.Y.L.I. at MENTQUE. Met M.O. & inspected some of the billets. Some were [illegible] into barns. In afternoon intended visiting 9th [illegible] Staffs but owing to message per [illegible] from ADMS went in car with O.C. 69th F. Amb. to S^T OMER. Returned at 7 pm. Weather, Very cold, snow.	[illegible]
	9.3.17		At 8.15 ready to proceed in car to 70th F. Amb. for lecture at WORMHOUDT. Stayed lunch with Amb. In afternoon to BOLLEZEELE for demonstration on water cart & travelling kitchen to 68th Bde. Tea with 70th F. Amb. Section here. On return journey owing to punctures did not arrive till 8 pm. Weather – Very cold wind & snow.	[illegible]
	10.3.17		Going thro' inspectors' reports & drawing up weekly sanitary report for ADMS. In afternoon to 102nd Bde RFA for demonstration on water cart at MUNCQ NIEURLET. Usual office work &c. Weather, milder, dull to slight rain.	[illegible]

Instructions regarding War Diaries and Intelligence Summaries are contained in F. S. Regs., Part II. and the Staff Manual respectively. Title pages will be prepared in manuscript.

WAR DIARY
or
~~INTELLIGENCE SUMMARY~~
(Erase heading not required.)

Army Form C. 2118.

Place	Date	Hour	Summary of Events and Information	Remarks and references to Appendices
	11.3.17		To 69th F. Amb. at EPERLECQUES to give lecture on Sanitation. Had lunch with ambulance. In afternoon & evening going through stores & equipment reference instructions to dump surplus kit. 15 men arrived for billets & rations as per instructions from "Q". Also 4 men from Salvage Co. Usual correspondence &c. Weather, fine, mild	E.J.H.
	12.3.17		To GANSPETTE with M.O. 9th S. Staffs inspected billets &c. went on foot. In afternoon on lorry to POLINCOVE to give demonstration on water-cart to 103rd Bde R.F.A. Ford car broken down. Censoring letters, correspondence &c. On return called on O.C. 194th M.G.C. re cause for a cookhouse. Weather, dull to rain, mild	E.J.H.
	13.3.17		Car requested from 69th F. Amb. did not arrive till I sent message after 10 o'clock. On ambulance to 70th F.A. WORMHOUDT but owing to delays too late to give lecture. Lunch with 70th F. Amb. Returned via BOLLEZEELE saw Lieut. Chapman re measles case 70th F.A. To RUMINGHEM to give demonstration on water cart to D.A.C. Capt HAMILTON present. Usual office routine. Weather, Damp, mild.	E.J.H.
	14.3.17		On foot to MORINGHEM to give lecture on sanitation to 71st F. Amb. Had lunch there. In afternoon gave demonstration on water carts & travelling kitchen to 69th Bde. Brigadier General Lambert was present. Censoring letters, reports, correspondence &c. Weather, wet, mild	E.J.H.
	15.3.17		Inspected 8th Yorks & M.V.C. billets at MOULLE. In afternoon to St OMER saw A.D.M.S also to field laundries. Inspected 192nd Co A.S.C. at SALPERWICK. Procured spokes & badges for Section. Weather, fine, windy	E.J.H.
	16.3.17		In morning on horse inspected 194th M.G.C. at ESTMONT & C & D Battys. 102nd Bde R.F.A. Billets unsatisfactory. In afternoon to EPERLECQUES with Capt Llewellyn M.O. 10th W. Riding inspected billets. Saw Lt 69th F.A. to tea. Usual office routine. Weather, Dull, mild	E.J.H.

2353 Wt. W2544/1454 700,000 5/15 D. D. & L. A.D.S.S./Forms/C. 2118.

Army Form C. 2118.

Instructions regarding War Diaries and Intelligence Summaries are contained in F. S. Regs., Part II. and the Staff Manual respectively. Title pages will be prepared in manuscript.

WAR DIARY
or
~~INTELLIGENCE SUMMARY~~

(Erase heading not required.)

Place	Date	Hour	Summary of Events and Information	Remarks and references to Appendices
	17.3.17		Drawing up Div. weekly sanitary report. Saw water cart 8th Yorks with M.O. Inspected billets with M.O. 9th Yorks. In afternoon to D.A.C. Carried out investigation with interpreter LACOSTE re supposed cases of diphtheria amongst the civilians. Censoring letters, routine &c. To 69th F. Amb. to [illegible]. Weather fine.	[initials]
	18.3.17		Dealing with charge against two attached men for absence from billet. To St. OMER saw D.A.D.M.S. re move. Detached men to move with unit attached to. Arrangements for move. Office routine. Weather fine.	[initials]
	19.3.17		Surveying HOULLE for sanitary scheme with Capt. [illegible]. Supervised loading of lorry & despatch to ESQUELBEC. In afternoon surveying HOULLE for scheme. Drawing up schemes. Censoring letters, reports &c. Weather Windy, slight rain.	[initials]
HOULLE to ESQUELBEC	20.3.17		Section moved off from HOULLE. Attached men (cinema men &c) under Cpl LEWIS marched. I proceeded on lorry via St. OMER where sanitary material was picked up & taken with us. Arrived ~~[illegible]~~ ESQUELBEC about 12.30 pm. In afternoon arranging for sanitary arrangements for D.H.Q. Censoring letters & usual correspondence. Weather Windy, cold, some snow.	[initials]
	21.3.17		Inspecting re sanitary arrangements for D.H.Q. To WORMHOUDT ~~Saw~~ Town Major re material for D.H.Q. Saw DADMS. Inspected Signals camp &c. Report on requirements of [illegible] [illegible], village sanitary schemes &c. Staff Sgt & party returned from [illegible] F. Amb. to Section. Saw Maire of ESQUELBEC re sites for latrines. Weather Windy, cold, some snow.	[initials]
	22.3.17		On with accounts &c. To Field Cashier, & to ADMS office. Saw D.D.M.S. there, he spoke re manure burning, laundry waste water, weekly sanitary reports &c. Inspected during day work in progress in village. Saw CRE & discussed re material. Saw Capt Bell re Ford Car &c. Saw Capt [illegible] & inspected billets. Saw DADOS re yellow shoulder straps for Section. Usual office routine. Weather Cold, snow showers.	[initials]
	23.3.17		Capt Bell down with measles. In Ford Car to HERZEELE [illegible] M.O. D.A.C. inspected billets also T.M.B. In afternoon with Sgt [illegible] inspected 9th Y & L. & also saw M.O. 8th Y & L & inspected billets at HERZEELE. Practically no sanitary structures existent. Usual office routine. Weather fine, cool.	[initials]

2353 Wt. W2544/1454 700,000 5/15 D. D. & L. A.D.S.S./Forms/C. 2118.

Instructions regarding War Diaries and Intelligence Summaries are contained in F. S. Regs., Part II. and the Staff Manual respectively. Title pages will be prepared in manuscript.

WAR DIARY
or
~~INTELLIGENCE SUMMARY.~~

(Erase heading not required.)

Army Form C. 2118.

Place	Date	Hour	Summary of Events and Information	Remarks and references to Appendices
	24.3.17		With Capt. [illegible] to WORMHOUDT. On to HERZEELE & brought back [illegible]. Saw Capt [illegible] at [illegible]. To BOLLEZEELE & with Staff [illegible] inspected villages [illegible] of 13th & 16th R.W.F. 38th Div. In afternoon prepared weekly sanitary report. Correspondence. Turned in early owing to not feeling well.	[illegible] Fine, cool.
	25.3.17		To HOUTKERQUE with Capt Talbot inspected 8th K.O.Y.L.I. [illegible] in village & C & D Co. T. kitchens [illegible] clean. Water cart inspected not clean. C Officers mess kitchen unsatisfactory, dirty. Trench latrines in use [illegible]. In afternoon inspection new [illegible]. [illegible]. Walked to see Capt. [illegible]. Weather	[illegible] fine, mild
	26.3.17		To call for Capt [illegible] with him to WORMHOUDT. To PROVEN & picked up Capt Llewellyn who is to act as D.D. San. Sec. during my absence. In afternoon to investigate civilian case of diphtheria at KICKENPUT. Several suspicious cases found. Capt Llewellyn to further investigate. [illegible] men. Discussing work with Capt. Cl. Saw [illegible] re diphth. case. Routine work. Weather	[illegible] Wet, cool.
	27.3.17		Called to see Dr WIEMAERE Wormhoudt obtained particulars of diphtheria outbreak at KickenPut. Further investigations. Saw OC Baths and visited Baths with him specially re disposal of soapy water. Inspected Z & Y Camps. Saw MO i/c 8 Yorks, 11 West Yorks. Inspected 69 T.M.B. reported OC Camp kitchen not clean. Saw MO i/c 10 Duke of Wellington – inspected L Camp. Saw MO i/c 9th Pontoon Park re cases of German measles. Routine work.	T. L. Llewellyn.

T2134. Wt. W708–776. 500000. 4/15. Sir J. C. & S.

Instructions regarding War Diaries and Intelligence Summaries are contained in F. S. Regs., Part II. and the Staff Manual respectively. Title pages will be prepared in manuscript.

WAR DIARY
or
INTELLIGENCE SUMMARY.
(Erase heading not required.)

Army Form C. 2118.

Place	Date	Hour	Summary of Events and Information	Remarks and references to Appendices
	28.3.17		Visited 194 MGC and saw MO re case of measles. Inspected S Staffs smokeless incinerator at Zeggers Cappel. Met Sgt Etherington at Herzeele. Visited baths, site for central incinerator decided on. Saw Town Major & arranged fatigue party to clean Lanes & ditches. Attended football conference at Herzeele. Visited 71 FA. Routine work.	TLL
	29.3.17		Visited Town Major Wormhoudt re placing estaminets at Kicken Put out of bounds. TM promised to see civil authorities. To Herzeele re Water Supply of troops. Saw MO 23 SHC on same matter. Visited source of supply Wormhoudt. Saw DADMS re Diph outbreak. Attended Football match 69–71 FAmb and committee after match. Routine work. Put notice boards on infected houses.	TLL
	30.3.17			
	30.3.17		To Wormhoudt. Saw TM re water supply. Explored part of stream being used. Inspected 207 & 214 Siege Batteries on Cassel Rd. Herzeele Saw MO 9 R I L re Diphtheria case. Football match & selection committee afternoon.	TLL
	31.3.17		Saw Dr Wuemaere re Diph outbreak. Swabbed 11 cases at Kicken Put. Inspected 102 Bgd RFA & battery & MO. Routine work & report.	TLL
	1.4.17		Inspected 70 TMB with special reference water supply. Inspected 70 MGCo. Saw TM Herzeele. Routine work.	TLL TL Saunders

T2134. Wt. W708–776. 500000. 4/15. Sir J. C. & S.

www.ingramcontent.com/pod-product-compliance
Lightning Source LLC
Chambersburg PA
CBHW081531160426
43191CB00011B/1733
* 9 7 8 1 4 7 4 5 1 2 5 8 9 *